A Fighting Chance

A Fighting Chance

RAY 'DUCH' PETER
WITH DAVID HANCOCK

JOHN BLAKE

Published by John Blake Publishing Ltd,
3, Bramber Court, 2 Bramber Road,
London W14 9PB, England

www.blake.co.uk

First published in hardback in 2004

ISBN 1 84454 044 8

British Library Cataloguing-in-Publication Data:

A catalogue record for this book is available from the British Library.

Design by www.envydesign.co.uk

Printed in Great Britain by CPD

1 3 5 7 9 10 8 6 4 2

Papers used by John Blake Publishing are natural, recyclable products
made from wood grown in sustainable forests. The manufacturing
processes conform to the environmental regulations of the country
of origin.

Every attempt has been made to contact the relevant copyright-holders,
but some were unobtainable. We would be grateful if the appropriate
people could contact us.

Please note that some of the names in this book
have been changed for legal reasons.

Contents

Prologue

'WE AIN'T GOT NO ROOM FOR A CRIPPLE BOY LIKE YOU,' one of the black kids said as I was walking away. 'You just slow everybody up.'

Another kid shouted, 'Oh, c'mon, let Duch come with us.'

'He's a cripple boy, he ain't coming.'

I turned on my crutches. I looked up. 'Who are you calling a cripple boy?'

'You … cripple boy,' he said.

'Don't you ever call me a cripple boy again, or I'll deck you.'

'Cripple boy … cripple boy …'

There was a sort of surge inside me. It sounds crap, but it was like a whole release of energy I never thought I had.

'You can't deck me, you little cripple boy,' the kid started shouting. 'You can't do anything to me, you're on crutches.'

At that, I bent down, let my crutches go and grabbed him full force at the back of his legs, on the calves. At the same time, I pushed my head into his stomach. He went down faster than a Plaster Caster. His head hit the floor so hard I thought he'd crack the concrete.

I scrabbled around for my crutches. Got one … slid it straight into the arm socket. I was up. I grabbed the other one. But, instead of hoisting myself, I bent over and held the crutch firmly fixed to his throat while he was lying on the floor.

'Good one, Duch, he deserved it.'

'Leave him there, Duch. Let him stay on the floor where he belongs.'

'Keep him down, Duch.'

'Anybody called an ambulance?'

I slowly raised the crutch from his throat and stumbled a bit as I put all the weight on my other arm. But I was up, and he was down. I took one look back at him and spat out the words, 'Don't you ever call me "cripple boy" again.'

That's when I realised if you bark loudly enough at the world it jumps back, just like I'd been doing for years when it barked at me. But not any more.

* * *

Clat … clat … clat … clat …

'Here comes Duch,' said one of my mates, recognising the sound of my crutches reverberating round the concrete walls of Lewisham Shopping Precinct in South London. 'He's got his new legs on.'

It was 1977, I was just 14 at the time, and the precinct had only just opened. Ever since a flying bomb had ripped the heart out of the town centre in 1944, planners had been trying to give it a transplant. And the precinct was the coolest and smartest one yet, which is a bit strange when you have a look at it now.

But back then it was the only place to be seen and the only place to shop. Not that shopping mattered to us. We never went there to do any shopping, we just used to hang out each and every day, moving from one end of the precinct to the other, dodging the security guards, who were convinced we were up to no good and used to greet us with that cheery old English expression, 'Piss off, you lot!'

But we never did. We were always there, usually around the Puppet Café, which we used to call the canteen. There were quite a few of us, and we recognised each other, but we were all in separate clans. I was a rockabilly. Well, if anyone could lay claim to being a total Gene Vincent fan, it had to be me. Rockabilly had that thumping, jumping beat that dated right back to the beginnings of rock 'n' roll. It was white man's music with stars like Carl Perkins and Jerry Lee. You see, I'd never really thought of myself as black, even though plenty of my friends were. I never really looked upon people as being different because of their colour.

On this particular day, I'd been thumbing through the vinyl in the local record shop, got bored and headed towards the canteen. There was a group of black kids hanging around whom I knew, although they weren't in the rockabilly clan and often they'd sneeringly call me 'the white kid' because I wasn't into rhythm 'n' blues or soul music. But it never bothered me. I turned away and there were a couple of my rockabilly mates.

'Duch, Duch, we're goin' up to Danny's. He's got this new Sun Records compilation of old Elvis,' said my best mate Mark Richardson. The King had died around a month earlier and the market was being flooded with his back catalogue. I wasn't that impressed.

As I was walking away from the Puppet, I saw this kid on a skateboard.

'Hold on,' I said, catching Mark by his sleeve. 'I used to have one of them.'

'C'mon, Duch. The gang are getting away,' he said and went to pull me.

'No, wait. Look at 'em. Look at them skateboards. I used to have something like that.'

'No you didn't, Duch, that's a new bloody invention. Anyway, you'd never be able to stand up on one of them. Now, c'mon.' And he tried to drag me away again.

But I stood there, transfixed.

'All right then, I'm off … that's it … See you later, or see you at Danny's … that's it, then … I'm off now, Duch … I'm off … Bye … Oh fucking hell, Duch, are you coming or not?'

But I wasn't going anywhere.

I think it was at that moment, when I was 14 years old, that I realised everything other people were going through I had already been through before. It was empowering.

'Your mates left you, have they?' said one of the black kids from the canteen.

'Nah, nah. I'm gonna catch up with them in a bit. Why, what you up to?'

There was always something going on with that lot. They always seemed to sit huddled in the canteen, plotting, scheming, or talking about the original releases of Northern Soul hits. I remember Gloria Jones, who had just driven Marc Bolan and his purple Mini into a tree in Barnes, South London. She was one of their favourites. They loved her. And her crash came only a month after Elvis went to the lavatory for the last time.

'Forget him, he ain't coming with us,' shouted one of the kids emerging from the Puppet. He couldn't have been more than 16, but he towered over me.

'You ain't coming,' he said.

'Where?'

'Nowhere … you ain't coming nowhere.'

I was really small, due to my deformed legs and and when I looked up at the boy from the canteen, it was like looking at a giant. So I immediately said, 'Oh well, please yourself,' with a half-hearted smile and a nod of the head. And I turned to go back up to Danny's. That was when I heard the 'cripple boy' taunt, and decided to take matters into my own hands.

Once I'd released the kid's throat from the point of my crutch, one of his former mates shouted, 'Gonna join us then, Duch?'

'No, I don't think so,' I replied. 'I'm going my own way.' And with that I moved off.

Clat … clat … clat … clat …

Within a few short years, that sound would strike fear into London's East End.

1

The School of Hard Knocks

THE ROOM WAS very dark. I thought it must have been the early hours of the morning. I had been in pain for most of the night, like all those other endless nights before. Just lying there. I'd been lying there for weeks unable to move, unable to do anything, just lying there day after day. A steel bar was between my feet holding my legs apart. There were pins in my hips, in my knees, under my knees, through the hamstring and on top of my legs just below the shin. And, while that painful steel bar kept my legs apart, both my limbs were covered in plaster of Paris which had got dirtier and dirtier and started flaking off as the weeks had gone by.

And then there was the itching, just under the plaster. The itching had been driving me crazy. I'd tried to get my fingers down through the top of the plaster cast to scratch, but I couldn't get far enough, couldn't quite get to the incessant, nagging irritation. So I scratched wherever I could. But it didn't give me any relief. Night after night, I lay there trying to overcome the pain, until a tiny tear would roll down my cheek.

I was five years old.

'Come on, Ray,' said the bubbly nurse bursting into the room. 'Today's the day.' As she pulled back the curtains, light poured in on me. It hadn't been night after all. 'Look, it's a lovely day and, by the end of it, we're going to get you back on your feet, my little soldier. You've been such a brave little boy, haven't you? Well, you see, it will all have been worth it. Now let's just get you something to eat, and get you nice and clean for when doctor comes round. That's the way, just lift you up a bit here, that's it. Now here, that's the way ... oh, Ray, have you been scratching again? Now you know you shouldn't do that. Whatever will doctor think? Your mummy and daddy will be coming to see you today, won't they? And won't they be in for a surprise, hey?' She went on and on ...

Ian and June Coward were my mummy and daddy and had been ever since I was born. I was given away to foster parents from the very moment I entered the world at Lewisham Hospital, South London, on 26 September 1963, with the name Raymond Peter. The fact that Ian and June were white and I was black didn't make them any less my mummy and daddy. I didn't realise that white mummies and daddies didn't usually have black offspring and I didn't care. Their beautiful house in Hither Green Lane was home to me as it was for lots of other foster kids who passed through their hands. I was a thalidomide baby and, while the shockwaves from the 'T' word stunned the nation at the time, and still reverberate round the world today, Ian and June saw me only as a little baby boy whom they could love and help.

Thalidomide – the very word is enough to send a shiver down your spine, with its images of children born with hideously deformed limbs. Yet, when it was first synthesised by the Swiss company Ciba in 1953, no one really knew what it was for. It was prescribed for people suffering from epileptic fits, but wasn't much good at that. And then they thought it might be OK for controlling morning sickness and nausea in pregnant women. That's why, although I have come to terms with what happened to me, I am still angry that the drug companies didn't conduct proper testing and research into the effects of thalidomide. By the time the scandal did break, it was too late.

When I was a teenager, I took a keen interest in the history of thalidomide because I was angry, bloody angry. And I still am.

Kids were born with some of the most hideous defects you could imagine – deafness, blindness, cleft palates, deformed arms and legs. Some kids even developed flippers that extended from their shoulders, or toes adjoined at their hips. And my heart goes out to anyone who has survived with those deformities, but it also tells me a lot about how strong they must have been to have overcome their disabilities and get on with a fairly normal life bringing up their own kids. Their courage is astonishing and it puts what happened to me in perspective. After all, all I've got are legs that don't work, that's all.

When I was born, I had two club feet which were malformed and bent in on each other. I suppose it was too much for my mum to handle, or maybe she had been told what to expect. But however it was, she decided she couldn't cope and, as a new-born baby, I was handed over to Ian and June Coward. Apart from the club feet, all the joints in my legs were contracted as well, which meant they couldn't move properly, couldn't grow to their full range. The technical term for it is arthrogryposis – now there's a mouthful. But the doctors assured my new mum and dad that it wouldn't get any worse, which I suppose was some comfort at the time.

I was happy growing up in the house in Hither Green Lane. It seemed so big to my tiny little eyes. There was a large garden to play in but, best of all, outside there was an old-fashioned coal bunker where my foster brothers and sisters and I would play this great game. We would jump out of the bedroom window, slide down the outhouse roof and see who could land in the coal bunker. Of course, I could only ever have one go because, even if I managed to land in the coal bunker, there was no way I could get up and walk away, so I had to wait until someone came to get me. But there was always someone to help. It was easy when I was very young because Mum would push me everywhere in the pram like other little kids, or carry me, or else I'd be in a pushchair. That was all well and good but there was nowhere I could actually go on my own. I couldn't even explore the garden on my own because I couldn't walk. So that's when Dad came up with the idea of building something to give me mobility. I couldn't have been more than four or five at the time, but it was the first thing that really changed my life.

Dad got a bit of timber, just a few feet long, which he planed down so it was beautifully smooth. And then he fitted four wheels on the underside, one at each corner. There it was, my very own transporter. Using gloved hands and pushing against the floor to propel myself, I finally had mobility and my first taste of freedom. I looked like one of those beggar kids you see in big Indian cities or that bloke in the film *Trading Places*. But that didn't bother me, because I also had, however tiny, my first taste of independence.

There were lots of foster children coming and going all the time. In fact, I was the only kid who stayed permanently with Ian and June, which is why I really thought they were my mum and dad. None of the other kids would say anything like, 'You're not my brother because you're black and I'm white,' nothing like that ever went on. In fact, the only thing that seemed slightly out of the ordinary was my 'uncles' and 'aunts' who would love to feel my hair all the time. They had never felt black, tightly curled hair before. I suppose I should have grown an Afro for them.

One day, I remember eating a bowl of custard, which I assumed was for me, but it was actually for another little girl who had just come to the house. I remember she caused a right row and started crying and that was when June decided to explain to me all about fostering. She sat me down and told me that she and Ian weren't really my mum and dad and that I was being fostered just like all the other children who kept passing through. But I don't think I believed her because I was there all the time and I don't think I cared about the other foster children, they were just kids.

Even if what June had said was true, it couldn't have meant that much to me, because I never bothered to ask who my real parents were. As far as I was concerned, it was Mr and Mrs Coward, and that was enough for me.

A bombshell came when I was nearly six years old. Dad took me to one side and said, 'Ray, it's time you went to school.'

I just looked at him.

He stumbled on, 'You must get an education and we've found a special school you can go to … it's in the country.'

I just looked at him.

'You'll meet lots of new friends and you'll be able to learn just like your other brothers and sisters.'

A frown creased my forehead.

'Well, son, don't you want to know more about your new school?' he said, trying to sound enthusiastic.

'If it's in the country, Dad, how will I get home on me trolley?'

'Ah, well, you see ... this is what's called a boarding school. You'll actually be living at the school, not here. You'll be in the country ... that's a good idea, isn't it?'

I burst into floods of tears.

The school was in Staplefield near Haywards Heath in West Sussex and me, Mum and Dad all went there on the train. I insisted on taking my trolley with me, just in case there might be a way of escape. But I took one look at the school and realised it was going to prove difficult to break out of. It was like an army camp, like a prison. I'd never seen a prison then but that's how I imagined it would be – like Staplefields. Since then, I've been in quite a few, and I can tell you I was right! That school was like a prison.

The first night, after Mum and Dad had left, I cried myself to sleep, as did most of the other children. There were about ten of us to a dormitory, which had no door, and it was cold, freezing cold. Totally the opposite from the warmth and comfort I'd known in my real home.

The only way I could get around from one part of the school to the other was on my trolley, until one day the doctor at the school decided I should be fitted with callipers and specially made 'Pedro' boots, those big things you have to drag and clunk along with. Although my legs weren't crossed, like when I was born, they were so out of line they looked like a bloody S-bend.

'We're going to have you up and walking with these boots,' said the doctor confidently.

So they measured me for the braces and the iron callipers, noted down how high the platforms had to be built for the Pedro boots, and a week later they came back to fit them on.

The pain was amazing, and the weight was enormous. I thought maybe they were trying to torture me. I hated the callipers and the boots, I absolutely hated them, and hated having to be forced to wear them and, whenever I could, I went back to my trolley. When the teachers found they couldn't cajole or coax me into wearing the callipers, they would try and force them on me and then, in exasperation, send me to the headmaster who would administer the slipper across my bum.

That was when I turned into a rebel. Whoever had been naughty that day had to stand outside the headmaster's office and wait to get a slippering. And most days it was me. I was completely unruly, I didn't want to learn. The only thing I did learn was how to despise authority. They would beat you and never explain why you were getting beaten. And that's how I learned about violence, the hard way.

After the first year at Staplefields, and with the callipers and boots proving to be a failure, it was decided the only way I was going to walk was if I had surgery on my legs to straighten them once and for all. It was drastic and radical because it meant having to break all the bones in my legs and feet and it would require me being in hospital for nearly a year. I'd always been an optimistic little boy, so I thought, Well, at least I won't have to go to that school for a year. But the pain I had to endure throughout the numerous operations on my legs was worse than anything the teachers could have thought up at

Staplefields. There were casts on my legs, pins in all my joints and there were tears – buckets and buckets of tears.

* * *

The nurse fluffed up my pillows one final time. 'The doctor will be here any minute,' she chirped on. 'There, don't you look a picture ...' And then the door flew open and in stepped the doctor.

'Morning, Nurse ... morning, young man,' he said, picking up my chart from the bottom of the bed. 'I see today is the day you are due to have the cast off. Good ... good ... mmm ... your temperature seems to be OK, nothing wrong that I can see here. Good luck, young man ... I'll come and see you after the plaster has been removed.' Then he suddenly moved closer and was staring at me. 'Wait a minute. Have you been scratching again?' he said accusingly. 'Really, what have I told you?' And with that he swept back out of the room. I then had to wait what seemed like hours and hours before my bed was wheeled to another room where they were going to remove the plaster cast.

'Don't be frightened, Ray,' said one man with a reassuring smile and a great big electric saw in his hand. 'You won't feel a thing.'

As the whirring started, I closed my eyes and gritted my teeth. I was seven years old and I'd been through so much pain and suffering with my disability and that horrible school in West Sussex that no way was I going to cry, no way at all.

Whirrrrrrr. The saw started to cut through the top part of the plaster. Then it inched its way from my right hip down to my toes. The soft under-bandage prevented the saw from getting anywhere near my skin. Then it was on to my other leg. I lay there rigid, too scared to cry, too scared almost to breathe.

Once the whirring stopped, two male technicians came at me with what looked like crowbars, which they hooked underneath the cut plaster and prised upwards. It all came off in big solid lumps. But the one thing I will never forget is the smell. It was the overwhelming smell of something that was putrid or rotten. Even the junior doctors standing around, eager to see what my legs would look like after all those months, started coughing and looking away.

Then all the plaster was off and my legs looked frightening. They were alabaster white and wrinkled like they had just been fished out of the sea after about six months. They were disgusting.

'Well, they look just fine,' said one doctor. 'Very good indeed … ummm … they look straighter than I'd really hoped. First-class job. OK, Nurse, wheel him back to the ward.'

And, with that, my bed was shunted back into the lift and taken upstairs. I wanted to shout out, 'Haven't you forgotten something? Aren't I supposed to get up and walk now? You promised me I'd be able to walk. I've been lying here for more than seven months.' But I didn't make a sound.

'Oh, you're back already, are you, Ray?' said the well-meaning nurse. 'I told you there was nothing to worry about, didn't I? All over in a few minutes, wasn't it? There now you just rest and doctor will be along again soon to see you.'

'But I thought they said I was going to be able to walk,' I said with a little sniffle, fighting back any tears.

'Oh, you will be, very soon, very soon. But, for the moment, we have to build up a bit of strength in your legs, haven't we? In a few days, we should have you out of bed and right as rain,' she added cheerily.

Mum and Dad came to see me. Mum had tried to come and see me every day but sometimes she couldn't make it because of all the other foster kids she was looking after. She always managed to cheer me up.

The days seemed to drag by as doctors visited, physiotherapists made me do exercises in bed, the nurse chattered on and I felt more and more miserable. Then, one day, the day I thought I'd never see, the doctor arrived and told me I was going to get out of bed and walk.

'Come on, Ray, there you are,' said one of the male nurses who was with the doctor. He lifted me up and swung my legs over the side of the bed. 'Now, I'll hold your hands like this,' he said, holding me firmly, 'and you just raise yourself up and put your feet on the ground. That's the way ... that's the way. Easy now ... there ... Now, Ray, I'm going to take my hands away and you can show doctor just how well you can stand on your own two feet.'

With a grim determination, I attempted to stand on my own. I bit my lip. I was standing ... and then, slowly and, it seemed to me, gracefully, my legs moved apart, further and further outwards, until I landed – bang – on the floor. I'd done the splits. I'd done the bloody splits. A huge grin came over my face, and I felt really pleased with myself. But the doctor and the others in the room weren't smiling. And that's when I realised I wasn't supposed to have done the splits. The doctor just slowly shook his head and left the room.

There were a couple more attempts to stand up but they never came to anything, and it dawned on me that I would never be able to walk properly for the rest of my life. So it was back to the Pedro boots and crutches.

My first pair of crutches were awful. They hurt under my armpits, my hands were sore even though I wore gloves, and it took me ages to get anywhere. Give me back my trolley any day. But I wasn't allowed that any more, and I had to return to the dreaded Staplefields with my crutches.

Although I had been away for nearly a year, my behaviour hadn't improved. If anything, I was worse, always getting into trouble and spending more and more time outside the headmaster's office waiting for the slipper. It seemed all the teachers disliked me and had it in for me. The only person who tried to reach out and connect with me was a woman called Mrs Anderson who seemed to be a combination of teacher, nurse and welfare officer. Anyway, she had a soft spot for me and kept saying, 'Raymond ... oh, Raymond,' in a lilting accent. 'He's not as bad as he likes people to think he is.'

Oh yes I was.

One day, me and a few mates decided to skip class and go and try to stroke the cows in the field next to the school. It was only when we got there and had a good look I realised they were bulls. But that didn't faze us. The others walked forward and I sort of hopped there on my crutches.

'Ray, Ray,' one of them shouted, 'they've moved the posts forward a bit.'

It was too late. My left and right crutches went down into the holes that were left where they had pulled up the posts. Crunch – I was rocketed forward and went face-first into the barbed wire, which was fencing off the bulls. Instinctively, I rolled my face to the left but wasn't quick enough to save my right cheek. The barb went straight through it.

I immediately panicked and tried to pull away but it only made things worse and my cheek was sliced right down to my mouth. The other kids raced to help me but the whole of my face was torn and my cheek was just a flap of skin pulsing out blood. I was in a very bad way indeed. The inside of my cheek was hanging out displaying an open wound. Thankfully, the shock was so overwhelming that I didn't feel any pain even as my mates rushed to get me back to school.

I was taken to the sick bay where a nurse helped to staunch the bleeding and an ambulance was called to get me to hospital as soon as possible.

That's when Mrs Anderson turned up. 'Cancel that ambulance,' she ordered. 'Raymond is not going to hospital.'

'But Mrs Anderson,' argued one of the other people there, 'this is serious. The poor lad's whole face is cut open. He needs stitches in that wound as soon as possible.'

'And that's the trouble,' she replied. 'Let the bloody National Health Service get at him and he'll have a huge scar down the side of his face for the rest of his life. He's still a young boy. I'll look after him.'

And she set to work. She held the flap of skin open and deeply cleansed the wound. By this time, the shock had worn off and I was screaming in pain.

'I'm sorry, it's going to hurt, Raymond, but in years to come you are going to thank me,' she said. But that didn't calm me down. With this pain, I didn't reckon I had many minutes left, let alone years.

And then she got out plain talcum powder – like unperfumed foot powder – which she used to dry up the entire wound while holding the flap of skin firmly back in place on my cheek. The pain was indescribable. I was crying, wetting myself, but Mrs Anderson stood there, firm as a rock, tending me. And she was right, right about everything. Unless you are really close up, you can't see the scar at all, but there it is running down from my right ear to my mouth.

But, as poorly as I was, I wasn't going to get any sympathy.

Next morning, all bandaged up, I was down outside the headmaster's office again.

When people spot the scar now, they go, 'Christ, Duch, what kind of a fight were you in to get that one?'

And I tell 'em, 'You don't want to know about it. It was one of the hardest of my life. They came at me tooled up with Stanley knives, slashed me right down my face.' I guess the cat's out of the bag now.

The authorities finally got the message that I was not the ideal child for the school and arrangements were made to ship me somewhere else.

*   *   *

For the half-term and full-term holidays, I had been allowed home to the comfort of Ian and June's house in Hither Green Lane. One day, a black couple turned up and knocked on the door. I didn't think much about it until I was told they were my mum and dad. Now that really confused me because, as far as I was concerned, I'd already got a mum and dad and they were fine. But so what, now I was incredibly lucky because I'd got a black mummy and daddy as well!

Their visit didn't really register with me, although, much later, when I got to know them, they told me they had been upset to see the conditions I was living in. It wasn't that the place was dirty or anything like that, it was the free-and-easy way in which we lived. I used to have a pet dog who slept at the foot of my bed and this totally horrified my real mum, who was amazed that dogs were even allowed in the house. The white culture and black culture are completely different as I was to find out in years to come. I had been brought up in a completely white environment and if things had been left like that I'd have probably turned out a lot better mentally. But, when Political Correctness started to rear its ugly head, Social Services decided they wanted to put black kids with black families and white kids with white families. And that's what eventually cocked it up for me.

The biggest blow I had as a child was when Ian took me to one side and told me that Mum wasn't well and she was no longer strong enough to look after foster children.

'What does that mean, Dad?'

'Well, it means that you are going to have to stay with another family, son.'

'But you're my mum and ...' And that's when it sank in and I started crying buckets as if my little heart was going to break.

Then things happened very quickly. A coach pulled up, I got on it and I never saw Ian and June Coward again. It was one of the worst moments of my life. I felt abandoned and alone. For the second time in my life, people who'd claimed to be my mum and dad had left me. I was moved around from children's home to children's home. One was in Bromley, in south-east London, and another I remember – a right shit-hole – was down on the south coast in Hastings. I had been practically kicked out of school, lost my mum and dad, and now I was being shunted around from one local authority to another. That's not bad, considering I was still only 11 years old. Things, I thought, couldn't possibly get any worse.

How wrong can you be?

I was eventually paired up with Tennyson and Muriel Rodriguez. They were from Singapore and had three sons and a daughter who were grown up themselves and were now working, and then they fostered a whole brood of us kids. Together, there were never less than about 13 people in their huge house in Lewisham, South London. But, while the Cowards had been loving and gentle people, this family was not like that at all. They had different values and didn't like softness of any kind. Weakness wasn't tolerated at any time. Their idea of raising kids was to toughen them up.

I had just moved to nearby Charlton Park School for the disabled. If you came home from school and had been in a fight, you'd be in real trouble. It was all too easy to get into trouble living there - if you came home and had forgotten to bring your coat home from school, you'd be for it. And dirty hands were never tolerated. I remember once getting my hands dirty at school and forgetting to wash them before I went home. I was desperately licking my hands all the way home to get the dirt off because I knew I'd get into big trouble.

If you mispronounced words you'd get a right mouthful. I had been living in and around South London all my little life so, naturally, I had a bit of an accent. Instead of saying 'isn't it', I'd say 'innit' and 'Pass the butta ...' And so it went on and on and on.

And fights were breaking out all the time. Every night there would be a scrap between the foster kids and the Rodrigez's own children. Life there was hard, but the scrapping did not bother the family as they thought they were toughening us up.

Every Saturday and Sunday, all the family would go to Blackheath Park. All, that is, except me.

'You can't come, you can't walk that far with your crippled legs and crutches,' said Mr Rodriguez, who used to make us call him Uncle. 'You'll have to stay here.'

And I used to accept it. But one week I decided I would go to the park. I'd never been that far before with my crutches but I was willing to try. After the first hundred yards or so, it seemed that every inch was one of pain. I started crying, but I wasn't going to give up. I was going to get to Blackheath Park and show them. So I walked all the way there, and I walked all the way back in tears. It nearly killed me but I had proved not just to the rest of the family, but to me, too, that I could do it.

All Uncle said, dryly, was, 'I can see we are toughening you up.'

Yan and Paul were into martial arts and were always looking for a rumble so they could try out their latest skills on us. They had been practising with *nunchukas*, the wooden flails that were popularised by film star Bruce Lee. They are just two sticks attached to each other by a small chain or rope, but they can be wielded tremendously fast and used to parry attacks from other weapons. Yan and Paul used to swing them around all the time, sometimes catching us with them if we weren't quick enough to get out of the way. I was very impressed by the weapon and wanted a pair for myself. So I decided to make a pair with two felt-tip pens and a bit of string. I carefully pulled out the bottoms of the felt-tip pens and threaded the string through them, then I put the plastic lids back on and I'd made myself a little pair of *nunchukas*. I went into the living room, struck the pose of Bruce Lee in front of the mirror and taught myself how to use my new weapon. It was incredible fun and I got quite quick at it. Early the next day, Uncle decided to call us kids into the living room one by one.

The room had white walls with big Chinese fans adorning them. And all over the walls were ink stains.

He knew immediately that I had done it, so it was no use trying to lie my way out.

'So now I suppose you are a *nunchukas* champion,' he said.

I remained silent.

'Well, the first thing you have to learn is to clean up your own mess,' he said, throwing me a cloth. 'And the second is this.' And with that he took out a proper *nunchuka* from behind his back and began swinging it around. He was a very hard, disciplined, strong man and that's how he wanted us to be. It wasn't a question of where we came from in life, it was where we were going. That was Uncle's attitude.

So it is hardly surprising that I was a disruptive and rebellious pupil at Charlton Park School. I knew there was going to be trouble because I had been taught to stand up for myself and fight. It started almost immediately I arrived at the school in Greenwich. The bully was a boy who I won't bother naming. I remember going to kick a ball about when he approached me and said, 'Oi, you, leave that ball alone.'

'What's it to do with you?' I said and ignored him.

He came after me and tried to swing a punch, but I just bashed him up. And I tell you, you wouldn't want to be bashed up with a pair of crutches. I could write a book on how to use crutches as a martial arts weapon if I wanted to.

After that, after beating the school bully, I was one of the most popular boys there. But not with the teachers; they despaired of me. Academically, I wasn't clever because I'd been through such a lot of emotional trauma and didn't want to learn. My home environment at the time terrified me more than any school or any teachers could ever do. I was a horrible pupil. I'd take my air gun to school and threaten other kids or even teachers with it. Because it was a school for kids suffering from all sorts of disabilities, there was no corporal punishment or detention or anything like that, so I wasn't getting punished like I had been at Staplefields. But I was getting plenty of it at home.

A FIGHTING CHANCE

By now, home life had reached a crescendo of sheer madness. And there was no going back for me. I was on a downward slope of violence. Ian and June had tried to bring me up in an almost Christian-like way, encouraging me to turn the other cheek. Turning the other cheek in the Rodriguez family would simply be an invitation for someone to take advantage. They weren't aggressive for the sake of it, but because that was the way Uncle thought kids should be disciplined. To him, it was a hard world out there and, if you were going to survive, you had to be able to stand up for yourself. It was no use being sensitive, that was just being a sissy. You had to be able to dish it out and, more importantly, you had to be able to take it yourself without flinching.

School was slowly becoming an extension of home as far as I was concerned. The games we played were all violent and, while I know most kids from 11 to 14 years old are boisterous and always getting into mischief, we used to go over the top. One of the games we played was called Nuts and Bolts. It was a very simple game. All you had to do was go up to another kid and kick him in the nuts and then bolt off so he couldn't get you back.

My best mate at school at the time was a kid named Paul Low, who was a bit more serious than me.

'Fancy a game of Nuts and Bolts?' I said to him one dinner break in the playground. 'You and me against the rest of them.'

'Oh, bugger off, that's a stupid game.'

'Yeah, well, I like it,' I said. 'And you don't 'cos you're no good at it.'

I was excellent at Nuts and Bolts because of my crutches. I didn't have to use my feet. I could just bang 'em one in the balls with my crutches and scarper away.

Paul and I had an argument about it, which turned into a bit of a fight, and I didn't see him in the playground at break times for at least a couple of weeks. It upset me a bit because he was my best mate. When I did find out what he was doing during break, it came as a bit of a shock. He used to sit in the class stockroom, where we kept all the books and things, strumming on an old Spanish acoustic guitar. He was practising something that Mrs Gillam the music teacher had given him to play and I was suitably impressed.

I wasn't in the music class at the time because it was thought I was too disruptive and I lacked the concentration needed to study music. So I begged, cajoled, tried turning on the charm, anything to get into the music class. Here, for once, was something that fascinated me, something I really wanted to do. But, because of my bad behaviour and past record, it looked like I was going to miss out. But I kept going on about it until, probably out of sheer exasperation, the school relented and let me join the music pupils. The first instrument I wanted to play was the piano, but I was told I couldn't because I had fingers missing and God knows what.

'You just wouldn't be able to play,' said Mrs Gillam. 'You need all your fingers … I'm sorry.' And she really meant it. Here was a teacher being sorry for me, which was a first.

So I said, 'How about the guitar then?'

'Well, it won't be easy … but it won't be impossible.' And she smiled at me, before finding me a guitar from school, writing down a few chords and telling me to go away and practise. Mrs Gillam was the first teacher ever to treat me like other pupils, and I made up my mind right there and then that I wasn't going to let her down. Instead of fighting at playtime, Paul and I would both sit in the stockroom playing our guitars.

I wanted to take my guitar home and tell Uncle and the family that I was going to be a musician, but even I realised how ludicrous that was going to sound. For a start, Yan, Paul and the others would laugh at me. So I had to keep my ambitions about being a musician to myself. But it kept eating away at me and I wanted to share the idea with someone other than just Paul and Mrs Gillam. So, one day, I left the guitar at school in case it got smashed but resolved to bring up the subject with Uncle and Muriel in the hope they might think it was a brilliant idea and buy me a new guitar.

All the way home from school, I kept rehearsing what I was going to say: 'Uncle, say someone wanted to be a musician ... What age do you think they would have to start?' No, that wouldn't do. 'Uncle, I've got a friend at school who wants to be a musician. Do you think he's a sissy?' Nah. 'Uncle, how much do guitars cost?'

By the time I'd got home and summoned up enough courage to blurt out something, anything, I was stopped dead in my tracks.

'I've got something to tell you all,' said Uncle, who'd made everyone gather in the living room. 'I've decided we are all going to go on holiday together back to Singapore.'

There was stunned silence in the room.

'We will also be going to Karachi and Malaysia and Vietnam. All of us, all 13 of us together.'

How much the price of a guitar now? I thought. But then everyone started speaking at the same time. 'When are we going? How long will we be gone? Can we skip school?'

It was incredible news and I couldn't wait to tell my friends at Charlton Park. They were jealous as hell, except for my pal Paul who thought it was brilliant for me.

I had a little calendar at school and every day I would

cross off the date and I would be a little nearer to going on holiday. I couldn't wait.

Then, just a few days before we were to set off, disaster struck. I was playing football at school, using my crutches as best I could, when a tackle went wrong and –crack – I heard my leg break.

Oh no ... oh no. They were pretty useless poxy legs anyway, but now it meant I would be laid up in plaster again. And worse, much, much worse – I wouldn't be able to go round the world!

2

From Pillar to Post

'DON'T BE SUCH a baby, Raymond,' said Tennyson. 'Of course you are coming with us. OK, one of your legs is in plaster, but it doesn't make any difference to you, does it? You walk with crutches anyway, don't you?' His voice rose an octave as he put on a show of exasperation for everyone else gathered in the room. 'So what's the bloody difference?'

And that was it. We were off!

Trying to get a gang of 13 people through Heathrow Airport – checking 'em in, making sure they go to the lavatory before boarding, keeping 'em happy in the departure lounge – was a pretty daunting task, even for Tennyson.

'Look, Uncle, it says "Delayed". What's that mean?'

'Just keep your eye on the screen, Raymond, just keep your eye on the screen.'

Eventually, we made it to the boarding gate – and by then we were all suffering from 'gate fever'.

'I can see the planes … I can see the planes …' 'Glen's got a packet of crisps. You're not supposed to take them on board, are you, Uncle?' 'Uncle, Paul's kicked me.' 'Why have you got that bag, Uncle?' 'What's "Duty Free" mean?'

'WILL YOU LOT JUST SHUT UP!'

Because my leg was in plaster and sticking out, I got a better seat than the others, which really pissed the rest of 'em off. I was special.

I can't remember much about the flight, but when we got to Karachi there was a war going on, which involved border skirmishes.

Helicopters were circling the airport. It was supposed to be just a stopover, but something had gone wrong. We were hustled into the arrivals lounge and told to stay there.

We did as we were told – for two fucking days! The lavatory was a hole in the ground. The whole place was made up of a series of tin sheds.

The next time we landed we must have been somewhere in Malaysia and Uncle decided to hire this minibus and drive us all the way down to Singapore. Another two days, but this time filled with fantastic hills and mountains, clean air and waterfalls.

Because of the plaster on my leg, I wasn't allowed to go in the pools we saw on the way. But if the bus stopped for a second, the others were all off to cool themselves in the water, while I was left behind on board. I'd hop out, and used to watch them all splashing around. It was a shame a few of them, like Dalton and Michael, didn't drown.

But, until that happened, we had Uncle's parents' home in Singapore to contend with. It was the most amazing place I had ever seen. Here we are, I thought, we have finally hit rock bottom.

Home was a large hut on Changi Beach and that's where

everybody lived. Around it there was a moat, and the moat was where the sewage went. In fact, we were encircled by shit.

In the hut, we had to sleep on the floor and, again, the toilet was a hole in the ground. There were no windows. So every morning we were out of the hut as fast as possible, testing the air. One day, when we went back inside, there was a total army of ants marching up and down the table leg in strict formation. They had found the jam jar. Not only that, they had managed to knock it over and smash it. And here they were carrying away little pieces of glass up and down the table leg.

I was fascinated by it.

I thought, God if we have to stay here any longer, maybe the ants will start carrying us off piece by piece as well.

But, within a split-second, we all shouted the same thing. 'Oh no, what's happened to the bloody jam?' fearing, rightly, of course, that there wouldn't be any breakfast that morning.

It was primitive living on Changi Beach and I couldn't wait to get away. There were big iguanas always scuttling away into the undergrowth and sharks that used to break down the steel nets at night which were supposed to keep them out of the tourist bathing areas. Every morning, really early, men would come down to the beach and throw the sharks back over the steel nets just before the tourists were putting their towels down.

I found all this really interesting.

Thankfully, our stay in the hut only lasted a couple of weeks and then we were allowed out on parole. We continued on to Ho Chi Minh City, although everyone still called it Saigon, for a sort of family wedding. The Vietnam War had been over for quite a few years and everyone was wearing flares.

Saigon was heaven compared with the hut in Singapore

and the wedding was posh stuff. It was the first time I had ever seen food cooked on a hot plate. I remember all us kids getting a bit boisterous and me, of course, being told to behave myself.

Then it was back to London – and the big news.

I had met my real parents on several occasions. They had turned up first at the Cowards to see me and lately, while at the Rodriguez house, I had been encouraged to visit them and stay overnight. I hated going to see them. But I didn't give them much thought. The meddling Social Services people had decided that care kids should be reunited with their real parents wherever possible – black to black, white to white.

'Muriel's ill,' said Uncle, 'and we are not going to be able to foster children any more.'

I thought, Hello, where have I heard this before? What's coming next?

But I wasn't given any choice and I was packed off for good to my real mum and dad who had this big house in Forest Hill, South London, where my mum still lives.

The first shock was when I learned that my father was a vicar, the Rev Jeff Peter of the Pentecostal Church of the New Testament. The person who had given me away at birth because of my deformities was a man of the cloth preaching love and understanding.

My mother's name was Rachel, although she was always called 'Aunt Bird'. In fact, everybody in my natural family had some sort of nickname. I had four brothers with nicknames like Kit and Blue and real names like David and Simon, and they were all living abroad, either in Jamaica or Grenada.

I had absolutely nothing in common with my parents and it was an indictment of how inept Social Services were that they thought I ever would have. I'd been brought up from birth by a white family with white cultural values. I spoke with a perfect white British accent and didn't even understand Caribbean patois. But no, I had black skin and therefore I had to be with black people. You can't get much more institutionally racist than Social Services.

I was immediately scared of my father because I didn't understand black culture and, although he is a strong man, I found him hard and ignorant.

I was given the pet nickname of 'Duch', which I immediately hated because it rhymed with the word 'crutch' and I thought everyone was trying to take the piss out of me. But slowly it started to stick.

'And how's Duch today?' Dad would say after I came home from school, because I was still going to Charlton Park at the time. As if he cared. If he had really cared about me, why did he have me fostered out from the moment I was born?

But I never asked him the big question, and he never apologised to me either. It was a stand-off. Only years later did I find out that he had taken me back out of care after being taunted and questioned by his friends who kept demanding, 'How come, if you're a priest, do you have a kid in care?' He took me back to stop the questions. But the big secret, the reason why he put me there in the first place, was to remain a mystery for a long time.

I hated living in the house in Forest Hill. All the children's homes I had been in, and which I detested at the time, were preferable to being with my real parents. There was a seething undercurrent of animosity between my dad and myself and he was the absolute ruler of the house. My mum did as she was told, which mainly consisted of cooking, cleaning and not expressing any opinions.

To take my mind off the atmosphere at home, I turned more and more towards my music.

The guitar was and still is my favourite instrument, but at school I couldn't just play that all the time and had to join in with the other kids.

'Raymond,' said Mrs Gillam one day.

'Yes, Mrs Gillam.'

'I want you to join the Wingfield Orchestra.'

'The what?'

'Wingfield Orchestra, Raymond … pay attention. They play and rehearse in Blackheath and I think it will be a great experience for you. You'll learn how to play music with other people.'

The Wingfield Orchestra was a local outfit made up of kids from different schools and a few very good musicians. I used to go along there every Monday to learn about different musical instruments and, if I was lucky, I'd get to play in the ensemble.

'Can I play today?' I'd ask the leader.

'Yes, you can.'

'Oh great, and what instrument have you got for me?'

'You can play the triangle,' I was told.

If it wasn't that, it was the tambourine. As you can see, I was getting pretty adventurous.

And then it was announced that the Wingfield Orchestra would play the Royal Albert Hall in Central London, probably the most prestigious place to play in the whole of the capital. It was a charity affair and, even though I thought the Wingfield Orchestra was heaps of crap and wished I were in a rock band, I have to admit to being both excited and nervous.

I had moved on from the triangle and tambourine and that day I played the kettledrums.

Nowadays, when I tell people I once played at the Royal Albert Hall, they just raise their eyebrows as if to say, 'There goes Duch again, bullshittin'.' But it's the truth.

* * *

Back at school, Paul Low and me were still making the music we liked and were out of the stockroom by now. In fact, we were so far out of the stockroom that we decided to form our own group which we called Vine. There was me, Paul, two girls and a drummer named Keith. Although we were rockabilly fans and loved dressing like Gene Vincent and Carl Perkins, that wasn't the music we played; we preferred modern pop and I was into Wings at the time.

Our big break came when the school decided to buy some four-track recording equipment to help with the music lessons.

'Mrs Gillam, can we record our group?'

'I suppose that's what it's for, Raymond, but you'll have to work out how to do it yourself. And don't break it, mind.'

We decided to make an album, or 'EP' as they were called. Paul contributed his song 'Yo-Yo' and I threw in the one I'd written, 'Billy Run'. For a crowd-pleaser, we decided on the smash hit of the time – 'Mull of Kintyre'.

'We'll never get away with it, Duch,' said Paul.

'What do you mean?'

'Recording "Mull of Kintyre". We'll never get away with it. It's a Paul McCartney song, mate. You know what he's like.'

'OK then, I'll phone him and ask him if we can record it.'

'You don't know his number.'

'All right then, I'll send him a bloody letter!'

And that's exactly what I did.

He wrote back saying he was perfectly happy for Vine to record 'Mull of Kintyre' and waved any royalties he might be due as long as all the money raised went towards the school. However, his busy schedule wouldn't allow him to attend the recording and act as engineer.

We were stumped; nobody knew how to work this four-track until we decided that the other song on the EP would be Squeeze's 'Tempted':

'Phone them up,' said Paul.

'I haven't got their number,' I replied sarcastically.

So I wrote to them and received a blistering reply from Jools Holland and Glenn Tilbrook who said they would love to come and supervise the recording.

It was amazing. We were still only 15 and there were Jools Holland and Glenn Tilbrook engineering us. They were either impressed or simply being gentlemen when they said they'd like to hear more of my stuff. Frankly, there wasn't much more. 'Billy Run' had a sort of 'Bohemian Rhapsody' structure to it, all changes. Well, you know what it's like when you're an adolescent.

The EP sold enough to pay for all the recording equipment at the school, but you know what? I haven't got a copy any more. I wish I had.

It was about this time I was fitted with my first artificial legs. Ever since the doctors had broken my legs years ago and found out I couldn't stand, it had been back to the bleeding Pedro boots. But even as big as they made those boots – and they were more like hiking boots than anything else – my legs were so feeble and small I was still only 4ft something. I had the height of a child when I was a teenager. I couldn't reach light switches, couldn't reach cupboards. The artificial legs would raise me to my proper height.

I was really excited when I was sent to the famous Cromwell Hospital in London to see the consultants about my new legs. But I was soon brought down to earth.

When the doctors saw me, they decided that the most straightforward way to deal with my disability would be amputate my legs from the knees and then attach extensions – to them it seemed like the best option as my legs and feet were so small and deformed.

But my mum and dad wouldn't sign the forms for the amputation to be done. As committed Christians, they believed God made you as you are and you should be grateful for it. Funny then, that they had given me away at birth, wasn't it?

The alternative was to make legs that could be shaped to my thalidomide limbs and so I was sent to a place called Chailey Heritage in East Sussex, an artificial limb centre like Stoke Mandeville. And that's where I met perhaps the most important man in my life, Dr Jonathan Florence. He was an absolute wizard who made legs out of this fantastically light plastic stuff, which is funny because you can't get that stuff today.

First my legs were put in plaster – yet again – and a cast was taken. A few months later, I was called back to try on this prosthesis they had made complete with a proper foot on the bottom. I had to use all these straps to get the legs on but it was amazing; suddenly, I could talk to people and look them in the eye on the same level.

The extensions cut the backs of my legs; there were abrasions, sores and blisters for about two years before my skin became used to the prosthetics.

But nothing, nothing at all could stop me wearing them. I was advised only to have them on for about eight hours a day but I used to keep them on for longer and would go mad when I had to take them off. They had given me a completely new outlook on life. Even when they broke, I used to fix them with an old coat-hanger and a strap. And they lasted me for a good few years. In fact, I didn't get them changed until I went to prison.

As the years have gone by, my artificial legs have become more sophisticated and the ones I wear now are made out of titanium and insured for £2,000 a leg. I get through about two pairs a year and go to a place called King's College in Peckham, South London. They take a mould every time because the prosthesis has to be a snug fit. A computer analyses everything, from how I walk to my body weight, and finally comes up with exactly the correct length of the leg extension. I'm now 6ft tall, which is what I would have been if I had been born with normal limbs.

But, regardless of how advanced my legs are now, nothing compares to the thrill of that first pair. As for Dr Florence, he went to America after only making a couple of pairs of his revolutionary super-lightweight legs. But I'll always thank him. He changed my life.

Back at school, I was literally walking tall and the first kid I made a beeline for was the school bully. He's dead now and you mustn't speak ill of the dead, but at the time most of the kids at the school were frightened of him. I remember once being punched in the eye on the bus by him shortly after I had joined the school. He was supposed to be the best fighter, but now I didn't have to look up to him any more.

He was public enemy number one, so when I got my legs I couldn't wait for him to start. But he never did. Instead, he sent contenders to have a go at me – and they lost one by one. They were a little firm of bullies, and as they approached I just knocked them over – bomp, bomp, bomp. So, if the mountain wouldn't come to me, I went after the main bully himself, and it was simple – down he went.

The other kids at school thought I was a bit of a hero and

I was really popular, especially with the younger boys, who had been in fear of the bully and his mob.

But at home it was still the same. I didn't really know who these people were I was living with; they were alien to me. My mum reached out, but my father didn't.

At school, they not only reached out, they started applauding. Whenever there was a school play or fête or whatever, I was asked to perform a song. But, when people finally started coming to see me rather than attend the event, I was taken discreetly to one side and told to 'bog off'. It didn't matter anyway. I was 16 and my school days were over.

'What would you like to do at college, Raymond?' asked the careers adviser.

'Rather not go, sir.'

He smiled through gritted teeth. 'But you can get a place at a tech. Make something of yourself.'

I just looked at him.

'Well, there must be something. What am I going to put down on this paper?'

'Electronics, sir, put down electronics.'

By this time, I'd cried through so much my life I didn't like to see a grown man do it, too.

I'd chosen electronics because I was in a corner. But I also liked it 'cos I enjoyed the feedback from the amps when Vine played. All that fnzzzzzz ... knaaaynaa ... knaaaynaa ... fzzinc ... and klnnnnnngzing. Yep, it was electronics for me. I mean, how did you get that sound?

And so my next move was to Nottingham Technical College.

'You're going away then, son, you're growing up,' said Dad. I thought, Wipe that silly grin off your face.

Now that would have been a good time to tell me his reason for taking me back, to let me in on the big secret. But he didn't.

So I slammed the door. And I breathed a big sigh of relief.

For a moment, I thought I was actually in Sherwood when I arrived at Nottingham Technical College. It was set in the woods and we stayed in these chalets – well, Portakabins really – in the grounds, six beds to a room. It was like Staplefields and Changi Beach all rolled into one. I thought, I can handle this. And I did. Most nights we'd sneak out of the chalet and the grounds, and go roaming. Not en masse, just a couple of us at a time. We'd get down to the local pub, pump ourselves up and try to look 18.

'You're under age, piss off,' the governor would say. So we went to the off-licence and then back to the grounds of the college to sup it.

Our nightly shenanigans were noted but nothing was said. But it all came to a head during a wheelchair basketball match. The team was moving well, in line. Gloved hands furiously spun the wheels on the chairs, then we'd stop abruptly by pulling hard on the spokes, deftly turning the whole chair and positioning for a shot. I was behind the halfway line when I caught the ball and it seemed there was just an empty half-court between me and scoring in the unguarded basket. I spun the outer rim of the wheels as hard as I could with one hand and shot forward at a mighty speed. My eye was on the net; my hands were on the ball, moving it up slowly, gently now, to make the throw. And then …

Slam dunk, some idiot spectator ran out of the crowd, right in front of my wheelchair and I quickly mowed him down. The basketball teetered on the rim, teasing it as the entire crowd held its breath. Then, 'Yeesssss …' the cry went up from the audience as the basketball neatly fell into the hole. But by far the biggest scream was from the spectator I'd mown down. 'Aarrgh,' he shouted, as two men with a stretcher approached.

The next morning, I was up in front of the principal.

'Peter,' he said, 'that young man's leg was broken last night. What have you got to say for yourself?'

I said, 'He walked out in front of me, sir, when I had a shot on. I couldn't avoid him. People shouldn't walk on to a basketball court while there's a game in progress. It's asking for trouble.'

'I agree,' said the principal. 'But you could have taken evasive action, you could have swerved out of the way. And a lot of your previous conduct hasn't gone unnoticed either. You know it is strictly forbidden to leave the college campus at night, don't you?'

'Yes sir.' I thought, Who the hell has snitched on us?

'Under the circumstances, I am going to have to exclude you from Nottingham Technical College forthwith. Do you understand, Peter? I'll write to your parents.'

'Don't bother,' I murmured under my breath.

'What was that, Peter?'

'Nothing, sir, nothing.' And I left the room.

I wasn't that surprised; a friend of mine had been thrown out earlier for something relatively minor.

I had been at Nottingham Technical College for exactly six months to the day.

Although my mum wanted me back in Forest Hill, I just couldn't go back there. I couldn't live by my dad's rules. He was too much of a disciplinarian and there was a lot of animosity between us.

Instead, it was another children's home, this time in Brownhill Road, Catford, south-east London. I'd lost count of how many homes I'd been in by now but it was beginning to take its toll on me. I started having these crazy mood swings. One minute I'd be really happy, the next I'd be in the depths of despair and depression and behind it all were these feelings of anger. I was turning into a very dangerous person and wavering on the edge of a nervous breakdown.

That's when my first girlfriend came into my life. Her name was Kim and I was introduced to her through a rockabilly mate of mine named Vince. At any other time and in any other place I am sure we could have hit it off for ever because she was, and still is, a very special person to me. Her parents were Indian and she was the most beautiful girl I had ever seen with flowing black hair and eyes that sparkled. But by now I was really messed up about who I was and what people seemed to want from me.

Kim and I did all the usual things teenagers did. We'd go to the pictures, hang around the shopping centre and listen to the same kind of music. Things would be going fine for a bit and then I'd have these strange doubting thoughts. I'd start thinking Kim didn't really like me; she only pitied me because I was disabled. And then the thoughts would get stronger. I started believing she was going out with me because she was warped and thought I was some kind of freak. Then I believed she was only attracted to boys who lived in children's homes or who had been fostered. My head was spinning with lies, delusions and half-truths. Her parents were very good Indians and liked her to mix with all different racial types. But then I thought maybe she only liked me because I looked black but talked as if I was white. And then I'd sink into despair and start thinking about suicide. I'd work out the best ways to kill myself – I could make it look like an accident, or it could be heroic and deliberate, or maybe it could look like I'd been murdered by someone else. And then the anger would start to rise and I'd lash out, breaking things and smashing furniture in the home.

Naturally at that age, my thoughts turned to sex. But here

I was even more confused than ever. I wanted to try and have sex with Kim but I didn't know how to go about it, couldn't get close enough to her to broach the subject. And then I'd think, When she sees me naked with these useless, freaky bloody legs, she won't even like me, let alone have sex with me. And so it became more frustrating and I kept thinking, What if I'll never be able to have sex? And then I thought I was doomed, and I'd lash out again or else I'd cry and cry until I became hysterical, throwing tantrums, screaming. The people running the children's home would try and restrain me, but I'd struggle like a madman.

Eventually, I was told I couldn't leave the house and that I mustn't see Kim again. I'm sure they thought I was going to hurt her. But I wouldn't have harmed a hair on her head. It wasn't Kim I wanted to hurt, it was me. I was just 16 years old and so completely and utterly fucked up no one seemed to have a clue what to do with me. And I certainly didn't.

So what happened? Because no one could handle me any more, they decided to move me to a special children's home at 99 Burnt Ash Hill, again in South London. And this home was just for black kids.

Can you credit it? All my life I had been fighting against this racial tag they had put on me because of the colour of my skin and now, yet again, the mind-numbingly incompetent Social Services had decided because I had black skin I had to live with black people in a black culture.

The house was run by a Mr Moore who, in his deep pantomime voice, would say very slowly, 'If you do not behave, I will remove you from 99.'

But at least I was allowed out of 99, and me and my rockabilly mates spent most of our time at a pub called The Squire in Catford. OK, we were under age, but this was Catford.

To get to the pub, I used to go on the bus; in those days, you could smoke upstairs but not downstairs. No sooner had I got on the bus than there was this huge commotion and this plastic cup came hurtling down the stairwell and hit the black bus conductress. She angrily rang the bell three times, the signal for the bus to stop immediately. The driver yanked up the huge handbrake and got out of his cab.

'What's up, love?' he asked.

'Hooligans upstairs.'

'Right, I'll call the police.'

While we were waiting for the police to arrive, I was dying for a cigarette. I reasoned best not to get caught smoking downstairs when the coppers arrived, so I headed for the upper deck. I wasn't thinking correctly. I hadn't been thinking correctly since I'd been moved out of Brownhill Road. The demons were still in my head, wavering between depression, elation and suicide. Upstairs, where the yobs still were, I sat down with my legs sprawled across the gangway. The police came piling up the stairs and one of them kicked me in the legs, really hard. Then other officers started attacking me, pulling me this way and that. I tried to defend myself but it was absolute madness. I kept saying, 'What's going on ... I haven't done anything ... what's going on?'

Then this girl started screaming at the police, 'What are you doing? Can't you see he's on fucking crutches.'

But all hell had broken loose because the police had immediately and wrongly assumed I was the troublemaker, while the kids who had really been playing up and throwing things around managed to sneak down the stairs and off the bus. I literally had to fight off the police in the gangway until they realised what a massive mistake they had made.

Then they started with all their 'You all right, son?'

Back at 99, Mr Moore, who fancied himself as a bit of a black activist, was incensed and said we had to sue the police for racial harassment and aggravated assault. He even went so far as to try and file a complaint on my behalf only to be told that the police had acted as they did because I was trying to steal the bus and they had had to apprehend me!

The implication was that, if we went any further with our complaint, then they would charge me with attempting to steal a red London double-decker bus. I mean, I ask you. How on earth was I going to drive it with *my* legs?

So everything was dropped and the incident forgotten, but it didn't prevent Mr Moore from grounding me for some reason, and so I was cooped up in the Burnt Ash Hill house all the time and just got more outrageous.

All the boys in 99 had to clean the house and some mornings it was my job to dust down the stairs. So I worked out a great way of doing the banisters by sliding down the stairs with one hand pushed against the wall, and the other on the banister with the cloth in my hand. But one day I must have pushed too hard because the banister railings started to fall out – clunk, clunk, clunk – all the way down into the hall.

I was horrified; what on earth was I going to do? Mr Moore would go mad. I had to think fast. So I gathered the rest of my mates in the house and told them we all had to go out and buy lots of Wrigley's chewing gum. We bought sticks and sticks of the stuff and spent ages chewing it until our jaws started aching. Then we got the individual railings and stuck them back in the banister with the aid of the chewing gum.

Everything was fine for a couple of days when all of a sudden I heard a yell, 'Urrghh, ohhhhh ...' And it was followed by a crash as Mr Moore fell through the banisters and hurtled to the hall floor.

Some time later, a seething and shaking Mr Moore informed us, 'I am removing you all from 99.'

And that was it; I was 16 and that was the end of my childhood. There was Trent Thomas, Rob Tyler, Freddy, me and Jamie Walsh all deported to Prince's Lodge, an old seaman's hostel in the East End of London. Whoever had made the decision to send us to the East End must have been mad because we would soon be taking advantage of everything that was on offer at the time – weapons, prostitution and drugs.

Clat ... clat ... clat ... clat ...

3

Lodging and Dodging

THE FORMER SEAMAN'S mission was, in 1979, in a run-down part of London. The old yellow-brick, four-storey building, with its imposing frontage on the corner of Commercial Road and Salmon Lane, is still standing now in the shadow of Canary Wharf, one of Britain's tallest buildings, and is overshadowed by some of the most exclusive and avant-garde architecture in the country. At that time, the area had yet to be developed; the nearby dockyards were in decay and you could smell squalor wherever you went. Clutching just a small case and my guitar, I must admit, even with my four other black mates from number 99, I was more than just a little scared about what the future would hold.

Prince's Lodge wasn't a foster home or a children's home, it was a halfway house with around 200 individual rooms and facilities down the hall, for anyone who could afford the

40 quid a week to stay there. It was home for the people who hadn't quite hit the streets; for prostitutes who needed a lumber gaff to turn a trick for a client; for small-time drug-dealers and alcoholics wanting somewhere to sleep it off. When it was built in 1923, it was an addition to the area. Now it was the last stop on the way down, and it was my new home. I had been shat on by the Social Services.

There were no real staff at Prince's Lodge. It was run by a guy named Phil Connor, who would go home after work, and a very nice Scottish lady named Liz who was Jimmy Boyle's sister. Jimmy was a gangster and murderer who had the reputation of being 'Scotland's most violent man'. He was arrested in a London pub in 1967 and, a couple of years before I arrived at Prince's Lodge, he had written his autobiography called *A Sense of Freedom*. Everybody knew who Jimmy Boyle was. Now he's completely reformed, and is a renowned sculptor. So I guess there's hope for us all. But back then he was a man with a reputation. And his sister was a woman with a heart of gold. Liz could see I was a little unhappy and scared when I first arrived and she took me under her wing, God bless her.

Prince's Lodge was crawling with weird people. Each of its rooms housed the sort of strange characters I had never bumped into before, and I was a bit frightened by them at first. There was chain-smoking Rosie who kept wandering all over the building asking, 'Have you seen my cat, young man, have you seen my cat?' although everyone knew she didn't have a cat. Then there was Lenny with these mad, staring eyes who just used to look at you intently but never said a word. Then he'd suddenly burst into hysterical laughter.

And there was anarchy everywhere, especially after 6.00pm when Phil Connor went home. The place would come alive. The resident prostitutes would be hard at work in their rooms, guys would be selling drugs and other geezers would be breaking into rooms to see what they could nick. It was completely out of control.

On the ground floor, there was a large television room and that's where me, Freddy, Rob Tyler and the rest of the kids from 99 would meet up in the evening before going upstairs ourselves for a smoke. One evening, as we were coming down the stairs, we heard screaming from the television room and, as we ran in to investigate, saw this guy high-tailing it out of one of the windows. Apparently, one of the girls had fallen asleep watching the telly and woke up with this geezer over her, trying to get her knickers off. And he hadn't been a resident at the Lodge, he had come in from outside!

It transpired that this wasn't the first time this sort of thing had happened and, apart from would-be rapists, all sorts of people were getting into the Lodge in the evenings. There were pimps coming to collect off their girls and even dealers selling weed from the Lodge who didn't even live there. Phil Connor had been aware of the problem for some time but didn't know what to do about it and thought it might all blow over.

'What you need here is a good security team, Mr Connor,' said Jamie White to him one day.

'Yes, I know,' he replied. 'But one, I can't afford it, and two, if the council found out what was going on they'd probably close the Lodge down rather than pay for security.'

'That's where we come in.'

'What do you mean?'

'We'll police the place for you, Mr Connor. Me, Duch, Trent, Rob and Freddy.'

'What, you lot? But you're just a bunch of kids.'

'That's where you're wrong. We might look like a bunch

of kids but we know how to handle ourselves. We've been brought up on the streets.'

Phil Connor thought about it for a while and then approached us about a deal.

'All we want is free board,' explained Jamie. 'We keep our £40 a week and we'll make sure the Lodge is totally secure in the evenings when you're not here.'

And so the deal was cut.

We hadn't been at Prince's Lodge very long, but I noticed that I was changing because of all the violence and crime that was going on. It was a common occurrence for people to report the doors to their rooms being kicked in and private possessions stolen. On one occasion, a man brought a girl back to his room where his wife and children were sleeping. His wife woke up and caught her husband having sex with the girl and all hell broke loose. We were out to stop all that.

The first weapon I bought was a Bowie knife made in Germany. It had a finger-grooved handle made of hardwood and a blade of about eight inches. I bought it purely for my own protection. We also decided to harden ourselves up in preparation for 'big trouble'. A part of the roof on Prince's Lodge was flat and that's where the five of us would go to train in the mornings.

One of our favourite films at the time was a Saturday-morning-style kung fu flick called *The 37th Chamber*. The movie combined martial arts with high-energy dance music and we thought it was so cool we decided to call ourselves The 37th Temple. The Temple would meet on the roof of the Lodge, which had no railings round it, and the idea was to force your opponent as near to the edge as possible before he gave up. If he didn't give up, then there was a 40ft drop on to a petrol station forecourt and certain death.

We didn't practise real martial arts like tae kwon do or ju-jitsu, we just invented our own. I had always been pretty handy with my crutches and now I was perfecting my style of using them as weapons.

We all adopted different clan names now we were part of The 37th Temple. I was The Cripple Master, there was Kung-Fu Rob, Trent was Bollo and Jamie was The Drunken Master because he was always pissed. But, boy, could he fight and, boy, could he run, too. There were some real scary moments up on that roof.

There was also a new guy who joined our team. He was black, his name was Steve and I met him at the Lodge. He went on to be a lifelong friend and I remember the first fight I had with Steve on the roof. He was using arms, legs and every tactic he knew to get me to the edge.

I kept thinking, Steve's taking this deadly seriously. He's bloody well out to kill me. He'd lunge forward, causing me to back off, and then press his advantage by getting in close so I couldn't use my crutches. Normally, I would go for the advantage first and use the crutches to keep my opponent at a distance where he couldn't hit me or make me move backwards towards the edge. But it hadn't worked. Steve had got in under my guard and there was nothing else for me to do but to back away. This happened a couple of times and I could see the glint in his eye and the slight smile on his face as he pressed home his advantage. He's bloody mad, I thought. He wants this to be a fight to the death.

I was getting very close to the edge now and, although I had artificial legs, I was as sure-footed as any able-bodied person. But I was caught in a very tight corner. So I decided to take a dive.

Down I went, rolling only inches from the edge of the roof. But it was enough to break Steve's concentration and

45

that was the split-second I wanted. I lashed out with one of my crutches and caught him firmly on the shin. As he looked down in pain, I brought the other one up with as much strength as possible and got him under the chin, forcing him to stagger back. As quick as a flash, I was away from the edge and prodding Steve in the chest with one of my crutches.

'OK, Duch, that's enough,' he said. 'But I'll get you next time.'

'You're bloody mad, you are,' was all I could reply.

We had all come close to going over the top on some occasions but that was the closest ever and I couldn't understand why Steve had not called for me to surrender when we were a good 2ft away like most of us did. It scared me and I didn't go back up on the roof for another two weeks.

I finally asked Steve why he'd taken such a risk and he simply replied, 'To test you, Duch, to see just how committed you are. That's all mate.' Funny bugger, I thought.

If anyone wanted to join our security team – and plenty did – then the initiation test they had to take was to come up on the roof for a fight and see how hard they were. Most would make it up to the roof but once they saw there were no railings and just a sheer drop they'd make some excuse and go back down again. 'Go and get yourself a job in Sainsbury's then,' we'd shout after them. That way, we kept our jobs as security men at the Lodge and nobody tried to muscle in on our patch. Pretty neat really.

I used to have a couple of side-kicks called Cyrus and Khalif who didn't live in the Lodge and were banned from entering it because they were always up to no good. But Cyrus, who was the skinny one, was desperate to get muscles like mine. As you can imagine, my upper body strength was second to none because I'd spent my life using crutches and, with the training we had been doing, my biceps were already starting to balloon and I was still only a teenager.

I used to arrange to meet Cyrus outside the building on the steps. One morning, just after I'd said to chain-smoking Rosie for about the eightieth time that I hadn't seen her cat, I walked out to meet him.

'Have you got any money for breakfast?' asked Cyrus. 'I'm skint.'

'Nah, I'm skint, too. Mind you, I know how we can make some money right here and now.'

'How's that Duch?'

'Watch.'

I'd stop passers-by and say, 'Hey, I bet you a pound I can do 100 press-ups.'

Most of them would just walk on by without saying a word, but now and again one of them would reply, 'OK, mate, you're on.'

Of course, with my upper body strength and my arms, 100 press-ups was bugger all. So I'd usually end up doing about 800 and then me and Cyrus were ready for breakfast.

I used to do it most days, and I miss those days because they were the best days at the Lodge. We had set up our security team and things had calmed down. Little did we know that things were soon about to escalate out of all control.

Lenny's staring and Rosie's lost cat were nothing compared to some of the oddballs at the Lodge. There was Doug who never seemed to wash and wore the same clothes all the time. He was known as Stinky. Then there was Maurice who was the total opposite. He was always immaculately dressed in a suit and tie and wore a bowler hat and carried a rolled-up umbrella wherever he went, as if he was on his way up the Commercial Road to go and work in the City. The only problem was he didn't have a job, rarely left the Lodge and just sneered at everyone. And then there was Queenie!

Queenie was what you might call eccentric. He used to wear eye-liner and make-up and dressed in a fur coat. He was obviously a man of means, treated everyone very well and said he liked to live in Prince's Lodge because it was different and full of characters. Everyone seemed to get along well with Queenie, to her face.

Queenie was in the communal lounge the night that Trent Thomas got into an argument with someone who was playing the pinball machine in the corner.

The first thing anybody heard was, 'What did you call me? What did you fucking well call me?'

'Nothing, mate, I haven't said a word,' replied the guy playing the pinball.

'Yes you have, I heard you,' said Trent.

'You're mistaken, mate, I'm just playing this machine.'

'Yes you fucking well did.'

And with that, Trent pulled out a machete from behind his back.

The bloke on the pinball machine screamed and must have shit himself. He took one look at the machete and dived for cover under the pinball machine. Trent brought down the machete with full force on top of the pinball table. The lights started flashing like crazy. Tilt. He swung the machete again, smashing straight through the glass.

In an instant, we were all up trying to restrain Trent but he seemed to have the strength of ten men. Eventually, we managed to disarm him, although he was still ranting and raving, while the guy under the pinball machine managed to scramble away and make a run for it.

It was later that we found out Trent was diagnosed as schizophrenic, which helped to explain a lot of things. He had been hearing voices in his head for some time and they had been getting louder.

Trent started a course of treatment and we went back to trying to introduce some kind of sanity to the Lodge. We all had individual landings to look after and mine was the ground floor. I used to station myself near the back doors because sometimes people from outside would try and pop the back doors open, get into the kitchen and nick the double cookers which were worth quite a bit of money. I also had to patrol the cellars underneath the kitchen which were pretty dark and come 1.00am it could get quite spooky down there. Many's the time I nodded off only to wake up and find rats running all over me. There wasn't a lot to do down there, so most nights I'd practise throwing my Bowie knife into the back of the cellar's green door. Sometimes Jamie White would join me and we'd draw a target on the back of the door. Eventually, we both got very good at knife throwing.

I remember once getting into an argument with a character known as Geordie. He was down from Newcastle and used to wear this full-length leather coat all the time. He used to think he was the top man, which made me wonder what he had done up North to make him flee down to the capital. Whatever it was, he never let on. But one day he saw me messing with my Bowie knife and challenged me, saying, 'You black guys don't know anything about knives. I bet I know more about knives than you do and how to use them.'

I tried to ignore him.

'Where I'm from, we're brought up to use knives. You blacks wouldn't know the difference between a knife and a fork.'

49

Regardless of the racist talk, I still tried to ignore him, and went back to polishing my knife.

'What do you use that for anyway, skinning rabbits for your dinner, is it?' he droned on.

I noticed that, although all The 37th Temple clan were black, I was the only one he ever picked on and I realised it was because I was on crutches and he thought me incapable of fighting back.

'Polishing your knife like a nice little boy, are you? And then are you going to put it safely away in the drawer?' he taunted.

'Look, mate, what's your problem?' I said.

'You.'

And with that, I threw the knife with deadly accuracy, speed and strength. It practically parted his sideburn, nicked his left earlobe and landed beautifully in the door behind him with a 'twang'! As he moved his hand up to his earlobe, which was bleeding, I grabbed one of my crutches and gave him a backhander with it as hard as I could, straight across his mouth, knocking out his front teeth.

'You got anything more to say, mate?' I asked politely. 'If not, fuck off.'

He never messed with me again and I guess I gained some sort of respect. My crutches were getting a lot more bashed and bruised than I was, and they were still my original pair. I'll have to look after them a bit better, I kept thinking.

The incident with Geordie made me realise that people were treating The 37th Temple as a bit of a joke and we had to put a stop to it. We decided we weren't going to muck around any more. We weren't just a little South London firm that was going to be abused. We had to start making money and we had to start doing this properly. We had to start being real mobsters.

We decided to stamp down hard. Many of the pimps used to get into the Lodge in the evening under the pretext that they were the prostitutes' boyfriends, so we decided to stop that. If the girls wanted to continue plying their trade, they had two choices: either they could go with their pimps and leave the Lodge altogether, or they could stay at the Lodge and we would run them. Many of them decided to stay and it worked out quite well. We never made a lot of money out of prostitution but at least we were on the take and the girls were pleased they had some sort of in-house security.

Not all the girls staying at the Lodge were on the game; it wasn't a brothel or anywhere near. Some, like Jenny, were there because they had been kicked out of their flat or they were down on their luck.

Jenny was a classy, young, very good-looking girl and most of The 37th Temple used to fancy her. For a girl at Prince's Lodge, she wore beautiful clothes and always dressed in a high-necked top, a choker or a lovely chiffon scarf. She was gorgeous. But none of us stood a chance because she had a regular boyfriend called Eugene who became quite a close friend of mine.

And then there was Sherry … a very pretty girl, kept herself to herself, no problem. Until one day she seduced me.

'You ain't half got a handsome face,' she said.

Don't look down, I thought.

'Fancy coming up to mine for a drink?'

The crutches were snapped into position in milliseconds. Remember, I was still a virgin at 17. The last words I remember saying when Sherry started taking off her clothes in her room were, 'Oh yes, oh yes please!'

On the business front we realised we had to take the drugs situation in hand. So we expelled as many dealers from the

Lodge that we could find and then took over the trade. It was nothing big. We would knock out £10 bags of grass or the odd amphetamine but nothing any stronger.

For a while, things seemed to calm down. We were raking in more money each than Phil Connor was getting in wages. Queenie, Rosie, Maurice, Lenny and all the other assorted weirdos started keeping themselves to themselves now there was a new order running the Lodge.

Then one day I thought I could smell smoke from the third-floor landing and went up to investigate only to discover the whole place was ablaze. The alarm went up – 'FIRE!' – and all bedlam broke out.

Due to regulations, there were fire extinguishers on all the landings and there was a fire escape at the back of the building. But the extinguishers were old and were never properly serviced. If you can breathe in a fire you can just about shout for help … just about.

We started banging on doors, grabbing people as fast as we could and directing them to the fire escape.

'Come on, Rosie, get out now, as fast as you can, love.'

'Oh, have you seen my cat?' she asked, a cigarette dangling from her mouth.

'No time for that now, love. Move.'

People were shouting and rushing around in a blind panic. The smoke was dense and creating its own havoc and the flames were roaring by the time the fire brigade arrived and got things under control.

Fortunately no one was seriously hurt apart from a few scorched lungs and blackened faces. But it had been a close call. Jenny's boyfriend Eugene had turned out to be a bit of a hero helping out wherever he could with no thought for himself at all. He was a genuinely nice person and we became close friends.

He used to take an interest in the music I was playing on my beat-up guitar. The starry days when I thought my old group Vine was going to be the next big sensation had been put on hold while I was at the Lodge, but my interest in music was still as deep and passionate. And Eugene shared that interest as well.

There was also a girl there at the time, a beautiful girl named Rhona, who used to love to hear me play guitar and sing. But, sadly, it never went any further than that because she had a boyfriend named Paddy.

One day, Eugene introduced me to a mate of his named Kirk who seemed OK but used to have these odd mood swings. One minute he'd be ready to go out to the clubs with Eugene and Jenny, and the next he'd be all morose.

So I asked Eugene, 'What's the matter with Kirk? He's acting odd now and again.'

'Doncha know?' said Eugene, looking genuinely surprised. 'He's on smack. But he's cut his habit right down. He's taking care of himself these days.'

Although we sold a bit of grass from the Lodge, we didn't condone heroin and didn't want the place to get a reputation as a hostel full of junkies. But there was little we could do about it except keep an eye on Kirk and make sure he didn't step over the line.

The second fire was also on the third floor but this time it was in an empty room and we managed to contain it very quickly although obviously we had called the Fire Brigade. The next day, a policeman came round to have a look at the damage. I didn't think much of it except for the fact he kept looking at me and I'm sure he was wondering, What's that kid got that big old Bowie knife for?

But nothing was said. He just asked a few questions about the fire and congratulated us on putting it out so quickly. He also started going over the previous fire which had not been so long ago.

'What did he want, Duch?' said Freddy.

'Oh, the usual bollocks. He's having a word with Connor about making sure the extinguishers are kept up to scratch and for everyone to be vigilant. He said the Fire Brigade would also be sending round some sort of inspector or investigator or someone.'

And then the penny dropped and we looked at each other with shock and amazement. We had an arsonist on the loose!

Everybody felt sick but we thought it best to keep our suspicions to ourselves rather than alarm everyone in the Lodge.

For days, I'd think I could smell smoke wherever I went and I even used to carry a blanket around with me I was that scared. And all the rest of the boys were twitchy and worried as well. We never mentioned our fears to Phil Connor, but we reckoned the police had already informed him of their suspicions anyway.

Who on earth would be nutty enough to try and burn down Prince's Lodge with at least 200 people in it? Well, take your pick. Here was one of the weirdest bunch of people you could ever meet. It could be any one of them. Most of them were mad as hatters anyway and the ones who weren't were pretty anti-social. There were drop-outs, alkies and drug addicts. Where do we start?

Then another shout went up. 'Can you get up to Room 158 as quickly as possible?'

There was a sinking feeling in the pit of my stomach. I grabbed my fire blanket and went to the room only for a wave of relief to wash over me as I approached the door. I couldn't smell any smoke.

But, when I pushed open the door, I was greeted by a scene of utter degradation. On the floor was a heavily stained and stinking old mattress with some of its stuffing coming out.

And on top of the mattress was the naked body of a man lying face down. His backside was covered in red welts and there was blood coming from his arse. Around his arm was a piece of rubber tubing and by his side there was a syringe. Scattered around the filthy mattress were used condoms. I took in the scene in a split-second. The room was disgusting with a filthy washbasin in the corner. I moved towards the mattress and, as I did, the door slammed shut. I instinctively looked round.

'Welcome to my humble abode,' said a person sitting on a broken old chair behind the door.

'Queenie!' I blurted out. 'What the fuck's going on?'

'It's young Kirk over there,' said Queenie in measured tones, pointing to the mattress. 'It seems he has been enjoying himself a little too much. He's such a lively spirit, don't you think?'

I moved to the mattress and turned Kirk over. I felt for a pulse and then looked in his eyes. His eyes were rolled way up in the back of his head, thank God. He wasn't dead yet, he had just overdosed. But he was going to be dead if we didn't get him to hospital as soon as possible.

'He's still alive, Queenie, come on, help me. We've got to phone for an ambulance.'

'Calm down, Duch. All we need do, my dear boy, is move him to another, let's say, more suitable room. This isn't the first time young Kirk has OD'd, so don't make it into a big drama.'

'But, Queenie, what the hell has been going on here?'

'Going on? Going on? Nothing has been "going on" as you put it. Kirk has merely been entertaining a few male friends of mine.'

I was still only 17 years old and I suppose a bit naïve at the time. I gawped. 'You mean he's been prostituting himself?' I finally managed to say.

'Well, that's one way of putting it,' replied Queenie. 'I prefer to think of it as gainful employment. Heroin's not cheap, you know, Duchy my boy. Now help me get him out of here. And not a word to that little tinpot mafia gang you run around with.'

'What's in it for me?'

'You will be suitably rewarded,' said Queenie with a half-smile. 'I am a generous man.'

Fortunately, I still had my fire blanket with me and so I covered Kirk in that.

'Queenie, in case you've forgotten, I'm on crutches,' I said. 'I can't carry him.'

'You don't have to, dear little Duch. All you have to do is go and find an empty room somewhere on this landing, get the key from the office, and bring it back to me. I'll do the rest.'

And then he gave a hideous smile, which cracked his make-up and showed his badly stained teeth.

The incident played on my mind for days and I wanted to blurt it out, to tell someone. I decided I'd share what I knew with Eugene because he was one of Kirk's friends.

But, just as I was plucking up courage to divulge my secret to Eugene, I heard the dreaded shout, 'FIRE, FIRE! SECOND FLOOR.'

I thought, Hold on a minute. I've just patrolled the second floor only seconds ago.

There was no CCTV in those days, and since the fires had begun we had been constantly on the move checking the landings every few minutes. If there was a blaze on that floor, I would have smelled the smoke earlier. I was there in seconds just as the alarm was being raised again.

'Oi,' I said, spinning round the person who was shouting 'Fire'. 'What's your game?'

And I was face-to-face with a neatly dressed gentleman in a suit and tie and with a folded handkerchief in his top pocket. In his left hand, he had a box of matches and in his right hand a match.

'Maurice,' I shouted. 'You bastard,' and I knocked him to the floor with one of my crutches. By this time, the rest of the clan had arrived and could see what had just happened. He had been caught red-handed.

The police were called and Maurice was arrested and hauled away. He didn't put up a struggle, he didn't say anything. He just went quietly.

He was taken to court but the case was mangled. It couldn't be proven that Maurice had started the first two fires, although we all believed he had. And I'd got to him before he had actually struck the match to start the third fire. He was set free and the first thing he did was come back to Prince's Lodge to collect his belongings.

'Get your clothes and now sling your hook,' said Phil Connor. 'I don't want ever to set eyes on you again.'

With that, our arsonist demurely left the Lodge. But, while he was crossing the Commercial Road, he looked the wrong way and – bang! – got run over by a bus and was killed. So there was justice in the end anyway.

Kirk had recovered from his overdose in hospital but was kicked out of the Lodge once Phil and Liz found out what had been going on, although they never knew anything about the male prostitution. Queenie's secret was safe. I don't know what kind of hold he had over people at the Lodge but he certainly seemed to have plenty of power.

I got talking to Eugene one day and I just casually said,

'I've got a strange feeling about Kirk. He was your mate, Eugene ... do you think he was a poof, you know, a homo?'

Eugene had a slightly startled look. 'Why do you ask, Duch?'

'Well, I used to see him with Queenie a few times and, well, Queenie's a right old poof, doncha think?'

Eugene was silent for a while, then he said slowly, 'Well, yes, it's true that Kirk's bisexual ... he swings both ways.'

He stopped again and took a deep breath. 'But while we're on, you might as well know everything.' And then he blurted it out. 'I'm gay, or a "poof" as you like to call it, myself.'

I was open-mouthed. 'Come on, Eugene, stop kidding. I'm sorry I brought it up.'

'But it's true, Duch. It's true, mate.'

'Quit joking, you don't look like a poof. And, anyway, you've got a beautiful girlfriend in Jenny.'

'I'm glad you think so ... shall we go and meet her?' he said.

And so off we went down to the first-floor landing to Jenny's room.

Eugene tapped on the door a couple of times, turned the handle and shouted, 'It's only me.'

But, instead of finding Jenny, all I saw was this bald-headed bloke just about to try on a wig.

Eugene turned to him and said, 'Jenny, I'm just about to tell Duch all about us.'

To say I was gob-smacked would be an understatement. From that moment on, I knew I didn't want to be in Prince's Lodge any longer.

Eugene got turfed out of the place. But it was mainly due to his friendship with Kirk and Phil Connor's crusade to rid the place of anything to do with heroin. Jenny, or whoever he was, left of her own accord.

Then the final curtain came down on me, too.

When I heard that some really heavy thug was looking

for me because he thought I had grassed someone up – something I've never done in my life – I realised my time was coming to an end as well. He started stalking the landings for me and asking people if they had seen me. I was living in fear and always on the lookout for him. Then, one day, as I was passing one of the rooms with a door that was slightly ajar, I noticed a glint of light reflected off a knife blade and realised the guy was waiting for me behind the door.

Quick as a flash, I rammed the door open, smashing it into him and forcing him to drop the knife. Then I pulled out my own Bowie knife and held it towards him.

'Get out of here now, if you want to get out in one piece,' I snarled. And you should have seen him run. He scarpered in seconds.

That same night, the big fish tank I kept in my room shattered and 100 gallons of water flooded the place and seeped through the floor into the room below. OK, it was an accident, but that was the third time it had happened and Phil Connor took me to one side and said, 'Duch, how many times have I told you – no fish tanks in the rooms. And how many times have you promised you wouldn't get another one? Well, that's it, you're out.'

And that was it. After all that had happened at Prince's Lodge, I was finally thrown out for owning a few tropical fish. You've got to laugh. Anyway, I grabbed my guitar and crutches and I was gone.

4

Firm Friends

WHILE I WAS staying at Prince's Lodge, I'd been earning a bit of money singing and playing in the local pubs like The Star of the East, The Five Bells and The Londoner. It was mainly wedding receptions and stuff like that and it was all done by word of mouth. But it was the first time I was actually getting paid to sing and I thought, Hello, maybe I can make a go of this.

I used to perform a lot of my own songs as well as the hits of the time and I did a mean version of Leo Sayer's 'One-Man Band', which was my main crowd-pleaser. I was still young and I suppose a bit idealistic, but I had these dreams that some big-shot from the West End would come down to Limehouse and suddenly discover me. But that's all they were, dreams. No Roller ever pulled up outside The Star of the East or The Five Bells.

In the meantime, I had to find somewhere to stay and, as

usual, Liz Boyle came to my rescue, letting me kip down in her small flat round the corner from the Lodge. It was OK for a week or two, but I didn't want to overstay my welcome, and I had no intention of going back to my parents' place in Forest Hill. I hadn't seen or heard from them at all while I was at the Lodge and, as far as I was concerned, I had abandoned them just as they had abandoned me when I was born.

The 37th Temple all went their separate ways and I didn't know what I was going to do next until Cyrus came to my rescue. He had changed since I first knew him as the skinny bloke who used to try and keep up with me doing press-ups outside the Lodge for our breakfasts. He had been weightlifting and training and was now starting to pack muscle.

'I'm in a bit of a hole, Cyrus,' I said to him one day. 'I can't keep staying at Liz's and I don't earn enough from me singing to get a flat or anything like that. Dunno what to do.'

'I might be able to help you, Duch. There's a bloke named Chris has a place just down off The Highway. He's got room and he's looking for some guys to help out in his business.'

'What's he do, Cyrus?'

'Oh, you know, a bit of this, a bit of that.'

'What's that mean?'

'Oh, you know.'

'No, I don't fucking know. Now tell me what he does, Cyrus,' I said, my voice rising.

'He runs a car-nicking ring. He's a jiggler. Nice earner.'

Well, I hadn't got many options. Chris was a big black bloke living with his wife in a block of flats called Brightlingsea Buildings. It's knocked down now, but back then it was right opposite Narrow Street in Limehouse where David Owen MP was one of the first people to buy a house. He spotted that the place was up-and-coming and got in there early on. I remember his wife used to have this funny sort of pastel-green French car, a Citroën 2CV, to run around in.

Chris was a real gent and let me stay at his place while I sorted myself out. He taught me about respect for family and, more importantly, the art of stealing cars.

There were half-a-dozen of us in the ring and we were all paired up. My partner was a guy named Bob. I loved him to death but sometimes he was always getting things wrong. I used to tell him, 'For a bloke with legs, you ain't half slow.'

Each partnership would take a different area – a couple would go north, a couple south – and we always nicked cars to order. Near Brightlingsea Buildings was some waste ground, which you couldn't see if you didn't know it was there. And that's where we set up our 'yard'. Between us, we could strip a car of everything in a couple of hours. And we would be able to sell the lot from the door panels to the bloody chassis, because of Chris's connections. It was a neat little set-up. Of course, it was a totally different sort of crime to what I was used to at Prince's Lodge but it was more of a challenge. The idea was not only to find the exact kind of car but to nick it quickly and silently, all the time keeping an eye out for the Old Bill.

Bob was what's known as a 'jiggler'. He would have a set of 16 or so car keys and, by experience, knew which one was closest to fitting the car he was stealing. Once he got it in the lock, he would jiggle the key around until the door opened, and then he'd jiggle the ignition. If he was on a good roll, he could break into a car and have it going in seconds.

In those days, and it's only 20-odd years ago, car locks were not sophisticated, car alarms were hardly in evidence and immobilisers unheard of. Car keys were little more than stamped-out bits of metal. So we all used to meet up at Brightlingsea Buildings at about 6.00pm – me, Bob, Joe, Steve and a couple of others – and get a list of which cars we had to take.

'What you two after tonight?' Joe asked me and Bob.

'Gonna try and go for the Mercedes 250 Saloon. The cream colour ought to be easy,' said Bob. 'And there's a couple of Ford Giveaways on the list if we don't turn up trumps.'

All Fords were known as Giveaways because they were the easiest cars to break into, an absolute doddle.

'What about yourselves?' Bob continued.

'Mmmm, wouldn't mind going for that Triumph Stag on the list. Doesn't even have to be broken up, got an order on it. Just a plate change and spray,' said Joe. 'Anyway, best of luck, see you back at the yard later.'

Bob used to rely on his hunches and this night we struck out for Greenwich and then Woolwich. Some nights, we would walk for miles and miles searching for the right car and this looked like it was going to be one of those times. When you are looking for a top-notch car like a Merc, then you really need two guys to go after it. Owners of expensive cars are more serious about keeping an eye on them. If an irate owner approached, then it was my job to divert him, threaten him, anything to prevent him getting near the jiggler. I'd have to 'bash the granny out of him' as we used to say. With me holding up my crutches, keeping him away, swearing and looking fearsome, all he could do was moan and threaten to call the police. There were no mobile phones then so he had to go indoors to phone, which meant we were away. Better if there had been mobiles! My crutch would have come down on his hand and smashed the phone in seconds. And if he decided to have a go then he would get what was coming to him. But few would risk that course of action; after all, they were insured and it wasn't worth it. And the fact I was disabled helped. Most people would think twice about attacking a cripple, so I always had the advantage.

'I thought you said you had a feeling about this Merc. Well, where the hell is it?' I taunted Bob.

'I've seen one around here, believe me.'

And as we turned the corner in Woolwich, there it was, parked, gleaming and shiny. And we were going to have it. Sometimes we'd spot a car which seemed the right one but there was just one little thing wrong with it and we'd give it a miss and carry on. Other times, you'd know from a distance it was exactly what you were looking for and this was one of those times with the Merc. I thought, Thank fuck for that, now we can go home. All we had to do was get in the car, drive it back to the East End and make sure we didn't get pulled on the way. Breaking in and starting up cars at night was easy. Getting away from the Old Bill was the hard part.

Bob got out his set of keys and set to jiggling while I was keeping watch.

After a few minutes, I said, 'Come on, Bob, what's taking you so long?'

'Any minute now, stay calm.'

Then he got out his second set of specialist keys and I realised this wasn't going to be the easiest motor to open.

More minutes past and I was starting to get edgy. 'If you can't do it, Bob, let's leave it,' I said sounding anxious. 'We've spent too long by this car. You know our rules – don't hang about, move on.'

'Almost there, Duch, don't worry.'

But I was worried. We had been there for nearly ten

minutes and that was way out of order for jiggling at night.

And then, all of a sudden, there was a car coming in our direction. Sweat broke out on my brow, I held my breath. The car passed.

'Right, that's it, let's go, Bob.'

And, as I said those words, another car came slowly down the street in our direction. The tension was getting too much. I started praying, Please don't be a police car, don't be a police car.

But it was.

'Fucking coppers, Bob,' I shouted and started walking. I thought, If they pull us, how on earth can we explain it away? Here was a black cripple and a white guy walking in the middle of Woolwich at 4.00am. And no dog! Fuck all, in fact.

Bob was too slow. He managed to get the keys back in his pocket so it didn't look like he was interfering with the 250 Saloon but they pulled him. As I looked back, I saw him getting nicked and the copper look at me as if to say, 'OK, let's go and pick up your mate.'

But before they started to approach me, I had turned the corner and I was gone. Clat ... clat ... clat ... clat ... Now I was going as fast as I could. I was heading in the direction of the Woolwich Ferry. I didn't dare look back to see if the patrol car was following me. They must have thought that, because of my legs, I'd be easy to pick up so they didn't put too much urgency into it. But, as I got to the roundabout, I saw a bank and a wall and, without a second thought, I jumped over the wall.

I could have been jumping into anything. There could have been a yard full of dogs, I could have impaled myself or, at the very least, landed in a load of stinging nettles. But, instead, I landed on a soft bale of hay.

I lay there trying not to make a sound, trying not even to

breathe in case I gave the game away. And the time went so slowly. I kept thinking I could hear a police car but I wasn't sure. The roundabout was nearby and early morning traffic was beginning to flow. I had no alternative but to stay where I was for as long as possible. The minutes plodded by, but with each one I thought, Well, at least I'm getting away with it.

Dawn broke and, as things got lighter, I could see my surroundings. It was some sort of small urban farmyard where local kids kept their ponies. It got to 7.30am, then 7.45am, and I thought the coast must be clear by now and so I scrambled back over the fence, dusted the remnants of the straw off me, and started walking down the road like nothing had happened.

Screech! A police car swerved into the kerb and out jumped one of the coppers. 'Well, that was a merry little chase you led us, wasn't it, lad?' he said, his voice thick with anger. 'Where have you bloody well been all night? I wasn't going to finish my shift until I found you. But I must say one thing, I've never seen anyone on crutches move as fast as you and I've been in the game 30 years. Now get in the car, you're nicked.'

It wasn't the first time I had been arrested. It's an occupational hazard when you're stealing cars. Most of the time I was charged, if at all, with 'allowing myself to be carried on a conveyance taken without authority'. This time it was 'collaborating in an attempt to steal a vehicle' or something like that. Most of the time I was let off or cautioned and it didn't bother me too much. I mean, I was a kid and I was a cripple; they were hardly going to put me in jail.

So we didn't get away with the Mercedes that night but there were plenty of nights when we got away with any car we fancied. And back at the yard, we'd be stripping cars and knocking out hub caps, tyres, anything you wanted. It was regular and interesting work.

Then, one evening when I walked into Chris's flat, there he was with some of his mates and they were sharpening their knives.

I still had the 8in Bowie knife and carried it everywhere but you never saw people sharpening their knives quite like that all together and in front of other people. Usually, you kept them cleaned and sharpened in your own time.

'What are you lot up to?' I asked suspiciously.

'Nothing for you to worry about, Duch, nothing at all,' said Chris. 'We've just got to sort out a bit of business.'

They continued sharpening the knives in a very determined manner and then, all of a sudden, Chris said, 'Right,' and all of them stashed their knives about themselves and left the flat.

The next thing I heard was a tremendous scream from the flat below. Then there was swearing, shouting, banging and more screaming.

Oh my God, I thought.

'Well, you can take that, you right little fucker,' I heard. 'Don't you ever lay another finger on my wife again.'

'Aaargh ...'

'And that ... and her ...'

And I heard a woman scream.

Christ, I thought, they're cutting them up.

Later, I learned that Chris's wife and the woman downstairs had rowed over the kids. Fair enough, it happens everywhere. Let them sort it out. But the next thing you know, the woman's husband got involved and Chris's wife found she was fighting the two of them.

Now that's not on. If the two women want to fight, let

them, but don't get involved. When a bloke starts on a woman, the laws change, and Chris did exactly the same as I or any other man would. You fuck with someone's wife and you'll get killed, you'll get put in a box. That was the law of the streets.

So Chris and his mates decided to cut up the downstairs neighbours a little, slash them here and there to teach them a lesson. As soon as her husband became involved, Chris became involved.

Because of the commotion and the screaming going on, the police were soon called and I think Chris knew that was bound to happen. But it didn't bother him, he still had to avenge the assault on his wife, even if it meant getting nicked for it. He was a man of integrity.

When Chris got banged up and the flat was empty, I decided to squat it. For the first time, I had a place of my own and, not long after, Sherry moved in.

Our little firm continued nicking cars even after Chris had gone down. Some owners tried to protest but, surprisingly, a lot of them fell for our line when we told them we were repossessing the motor because they hadn't kept up the finance payments. Amazingly, a lot of people hadn't.

One night, me and Bob were heading back to the yard in a crappy old cheap Vauxhall, I think it was, when once again we were pulled over by the Old Bill. It was the usual thing.

'Your car?'

'Yeah, my car.'

'Your tyres?

'Yeah, my tyres.'

'Your steering wheel?'

'Oh come on, officer, what's all this about?'

I'd dropped my Bowie knife behind the seat when I saw

the police car approaching, just in case. Now the officers were circling the Vauxhall and so I slid my hand down to pick the knife back up.

'Don't move,' one of the coppers shouted. 'He's got a knife … he's got a knife.'

Me and Bob were hauled out of the car and thrown roughly up against it.

'We know your game, we know who you are,' said the other policeman. 'You're from Brightlingsea Buildings, aren't you?'

Neither of us said a word.

'Is this your knife?' he continued, pointing to the Bowie.

Again silence.

'Right, you two are coming down the station.'

When we got to the police station, we were in for a surprise. There were two other guys from our firm already there, a white guy and a mixed-race kid.

We were all put in this one room, which had just a table, and the humiliation began. Because of my disability, they got me a chair.

Then this officer turned to the mixed-race kid and snarled, 'Strip off. I want to see you naked. I want to see your black arse naked.'

Then the copper systematically began to ridicule the kid in front of us all, in front of his mates. He kicked him, screamed at him, 'You fucking worthless black bastard,' and slapped him around the face. 'What's your name, kid?' and then another slap. 'What's your fucking name, nigger?' The abuse got heavier and, when one of the other kids tried to intervene, he was shouted down.

'Wait your fucking turn, you. You've got yours to come. Now strip naked.'

The mixed-race kid started crying in front of us all as they continued to taunt him. 'Black bastard, black bastard.' Slap.

They broke each of my mates down. They abused Bob, and they spat in the white guy's face.

That night, I learned a lot about what goes on inside police stations and especially what black people have to go through. It was only years later that the Metropolitan Police were branded institutionally racist. I don't know why it took so long for everyone to catch on.

Something had happened to me in an hour of watching this abuse and, when it was my turn, I got on my crutches and walked slowly towards the table. I stared the copper straight in the eyes.

'How come you're so fucking cool,' he said, sensing he was getting a different reaction here from the three people he had just beaten up.

I wasn't going to be intimidated and I just stared at the copper and his mate.

They didn't call me a black bastard; they didn't ask me to strip naked and they didn't slap me in the face and beat me. And they didn't do it because they were afraid. They knew, if they had tried it on with me, I would have killed them and damn the consequences. I just stared at them with as much arrogance and disdain as I could muster. These people were no threat to me.

They just kept saying to me over and over again, 'Would you have used that knife? Would you have used that knife?'

Of course I would have used it, but not on police officers. It was purely for protection. But coppers don't understand that. They see a knife and immediately think it is going to be used as a weapon. That's how their minds work because all they can do themselves is be violent, as I had just witnessed.

How can you let a police officer slap you in the face and call you a black bastard just because he is wearing a uniform? If someone did that to you down the road or in the pub, you'd knock them out. That would be the natural reaction. But the police hide behind their uniforms.

I wasn't yet 18 years old and I was charged with 'possessing an offensive weapon in a public place' and the usual 'allowing myself to be carried on a conveyance taken without authority', my favourite.

I was given a conditional discharge for two years.

I wasn't afraid of the police and, slowly, they began to realise it. On one occasion, when I was at home, I looked out of the window and the Old Bill were caning this guy. They were really mashing him. There were lots of other people around but no one was taking any notice, they didn't want to get involved.

So I raced down the stairs and went up to the coppers. 'Hey, you,' I said, 'leave him alone.'

'You mind your own business.'

'Fuck you.'

'You swear again and we are going to nick you.'

'Fuck you.'

And suddenly it was me they decided to pick on. The other geezer was pretty battered anyway so they just let him drop, and went for me. But, if they thought a cripple was going to be an easy target, they had got it wrong. One of them tried to restrain me while his mate fished out the cuffs.

'Don't touch me,' I warned them.

But they didn't listen and, as they both came at me, I used the force of my upper body strength to swing my legs high in the air, just using my crutches for support. Out shot the legs connecting firmly with each of the officer's chests, one after another, and down they both went. But they had a back-up van round the corner and suddenly there were another three on me. I moved agilely and kept them at bay with the length of my crutches. Bop! One of the crutches got a copper full-force in the shoulder and he yelped in agony. They were half-circling me now and trying to hem me in against the wall. When they finally got me in the back of the van they would throw me on the floor and say, 'If you move an inch, we will stamp you out.'

I used to fight the Old Bill and get carted away just about every other day and I can tell you there was more than enough fight in this dog. I got fed up going home with no shirt and beaten to fuck, but I'd never let them break me. They just used to sling me in a cell and then let me go. I got quite a reputation with them and even a bit of I respect, I think, because they used to call me Hercules. And I know for a fact they used to send their young officers down to try and deal with me, just to give the youngsters a fright.

The only copper that could talk to me then was Ray, good old Ray. He was the best copper I've known; they don't make them like him any more. Good old Ray.

But I never figured out at the time why the Old Bill never charged me or took me to court for all these police fights. But then I suppose in court it wouldn't look that good for the coppers when the magistrate had to say, 'Are you telling me that it took eight uniformed police officers to try and restrain one disabled man on crutches?'

Under my influence, all the guys in our little firm of car thieves were beginning to get hardened and stand up for themselves. I guess they thought, if Duch can do it, we can.

Since Chris had gone down, we had to find another guy to buy the car parts off us and we couldn't be too choosy. The bloke we got involved with lived down the other side of the estate and he was a horrible person, but things were getting tough and we were all having to work harder.

One night, me and Bob managed to get back with a motor just in time to hear this row going on between our new contact and Joe. Evidently, the bloke had demanded a certain part of a car, I forget what it was now, but Joe had already sold it to someone else.

'Well, go back and fucking get it,' he snapped at Joe, jumping out of his chair.

'I'm not going.'

Then the big bully slapped Joe in the face. 'Go back and get the fucking part,' he screamed.

'I'm not going.'

I have to take my shades off to Joe because the other guy kicked the shit out of him. But that's when I saw the determination of a small guy up against a big bruiser and realised the whole gang was hardening up. Joe refused to go back and break a deal he had already done. Good man. It's not the size of the dog in the fight, it's the size of the fight in the dog.

The amount of money we were getting for the car parts was falling and we had taken to nicking cars nearer home which was more dangerous for us but it guaranteed a higher turnover than walking for hours and hours in far-off parts of London.

One day, one of the blokes said to me, 'Duch, you ought to have a motor of your own.' And I thought, Why not? He had this mate, whom he said was totally legit, and he was selling this old Marina for 60 quid. So I bought it.

I had never passed a test or even driven a car in my life, which is why I always wondered when I got busted for 'being carried on a conveyance taken without authority' why I automatically got my licence endorsed. I hadn't got a bloody licence! Or tax or insurance or any of that stuff.

I didn't worry too much about not being able to drive

because I thought, if a pin-head like my mate Bob could drive, it couldn't be that difficult.

So I jumped in, closed the door, started the car up and then it suddenly lurched backwards; then it lurched forwards and then it settled down, and I just about managed to get the car moving.

I was going around the estate slowly and I thought I was driving very convincingly for a disabled person who had never been behind a wheel before. So I thought, Fuck it, I'll take it out on the road.

Just off Narrow Street there was a huge road simply called The Highway along which cars whizzed up and down at breathtaking speeds day and night. It was the main artery into Canary Wharf and Docklands. So I thought I'd just ease out on to it and do a bit of real driving.

As I looked right to pull out on to The Highway, I saw another car coming at high speed. But, instead of hitting the brake to wait, my foot caught the accelerator and I lurched forward and started moving into the road. The other car was getting closer and closer. I couldn't get my artificial leg off the accelerator. The driver hit his horn but there was nothing I could do and I thought that was it. But then he whizzed past me, horn at full blast, missing the Marina by a hair's breadth. But I didn't have time to think how lucky I was because now I was on the opposite side of the road with cars coming from the left. Oh Christ! With my foot stuck on the accelerator, I jammed it down and turned the steering wheel fully clockwise. I did a complete turn and was off The Highway and heading back down Narrow Street after the fright of my life.

As I was going down Narrow Street, I tried everything from pulling on the handbrake to throwing the car into reverse, but my foot was still stuck on the accelerator and the car was out of control.

That's when I saw this pastel green French car, a Citroën 2CV, parked outside a pub called The Grapes. Smash, I went straight into the back of the 2CV and shuddered to a halt.

I got out of the car as best I could and tried to high-tail it home when I heard this booming voice, 'Come here, lad, you can't run away from a thing like this.' I turned and recognised Dr David Owen MP. 'That's my wife's car you have just smashed up,' he said.

At that point, some smart guy came out of the pub and started mouthing off, 'He nicked that car, he nicked that Marina. He's in with a whole gang of them.'

I shouted at the bloke, 'Fuck off or I'll punch your lights out. I never nicked that car, I bought it. It's mine all right, it cost me 60 quid.'

David Owen, being an upstanding politician, reported the whole affair to the police. His wife's car was a complete write-off and, once more, the coppers were on my case.

At the time, the pressure was still on us to nick as many cars as quickly as possible to provide an ever-increasing demand for spare parts. One day I said to Bob, 'We need a car quickly, mate. Go and get one as quick as you can. Go on your own.'

Off he went and he was back in a flash.

'Bloody hell, Bob,' I said. 'I've always been having a dig at you for being so slow but you've proved me wrong today. Nice one, mate. Where did you get the motor?'

'Down the West India Dock Road.'

'The fucking West India Dock Road? Where Limehouse Police Station is?'

'Yeah, Duch.'

'Whereabouts down there?'

'Right by the station, Duch. Easiest one ever, keys still in it.'

My heart sank.

The police were round at Brightlingsea Buildings almost as fast as Bob, and a long time before we had time to strip the bright, shiny new red car from West India Dock Road.

'You've all gone too far this time,' said one police officer. 'He's gone mad, he's gone bloody ballistic. Now tell me, which one of you bright sparks thought it would be fun to nick the Chief Superintendent's brand-new car?'

I realised we were in deep shit but none of us could help but snigger when we realised just what Bob had done. The image of the Chief Super coming out of the station to go home to his wife and kids only to find his car stolen from under his nose made us all crack up.

The whole firm came crumbling down after that and we all ended up in court. On the surface, they were fairly trivial offences and smashing up the Citroën was treated no more severely than a normal car accident. But it was the stature of the people involved, David Owen and the local Chief Superintendent, which forced the magistrates to have a long hard look at our records.

The police were determined to nail us completely. They wanted nothing less than Hercules behind bars. So, when my case came up, I thought it was likely that the coppers would oppose bail – and they did. And so I was remanded in custody. I was going down for the first time.

The thing about going down is that you're never quite prepared for it. Never quite prepared for not going home. I kept thinking about silly things like forgetting to feed the dog before I left for court, and not leaving a note saying I wouldn't be back.

5

Going to the Dogs

CLAT ... CLAT ... CLAT ... CLAT ... I was going down.
I conked out when I got to the Latchmere House borstal
in Richmond, Surrey. I'd had the 'flu very badly for days,
and when the magistrate said, 'I'm Mr Friend, only by name
and not by nature,' I was convinced I was going down. I'd
already been up before him, and he'd threatened me then
with his 'don't-want-to-see-you-in-this-court-again' speech.

The 'flu had got a grip and, by the time I got to Latchmere,
my mind was in a spin. The only thing I could focus on was
my dog, Chub. What was going to happen to him?

I'd bought Chub from a friend of mine called Omara while
I was living in Brightlingsea Buildings, although I'd known
Omara since Prince's Lodge days. He was the son of an Arab
diplomat, very cocky and had more money than us. The
girls loved him and you could mistake him for a very flash
black guy. But because of his fast-living lifestyle – he used

to hang out all the time at a pub called Charlie Brown's – one day he would be loaded and the next day he would be broke. I bumped into him one day down the dole office and he had his dog Chub with him, a cross between a Doberman and a German Shepherd.

Seeing that Omara was skint again and I was on my own and needed a friend, I offered him a tenner for the dog.

'Fifteen,' he said.

'Haven't got it.'

'Can't have the dog then.' And he walked away.

But I wanted the dog so much that I went back home and ponced a fiver off someone, tracked Omara down and got him to agree to sell me the dog. Now I had a friend.

But here I was, 'flued up to the eyeballs in Latchmere House and there was no one at home to look after Chub and feed him. Because the dog had been treated so indifferently by Omara as a youngster, he was quite vicious and I had to keep him indoors all day and only exercise him at night when there weren't that many other dogs around.

I was shivering, sweating and worrying about Chub when one of the screws said it was OK for me to make a phone call. So I called a friend of mine named Linda, who also used to hang around at Charlie Brown's pub, and she went round to Brightlingsea Buildings and grabbed the dog. I'll always be thankful to her for that.

My mind was at rest but my brain was still on fire with the 'flu. Latchmere House was a horrible nick. They gave me a blue uniform to wear and kept on telling me to go for 'association' – they didn't call it exercise then – which mainly consisted of me sitting in the TV room shivering to death.

What I didn't know at the time was that the screws were desperate to get me moved because there were no facilities for the disabled at Latchmere and most of the staff didn't know how to treat me. Should they be as harsh on me as they were with the able-bodied lads or should they cut corners and make exceptions because of my thalidomide legs? It was a dilemma I was to notice again and again throughout my years in Her Majesty's prisons.

After a couple of weeks, I was up for bail again at the court round the back of Arbour Square off Commercial Road in East London, and again I was sent back to Latchmere House. My 'flu had thankfully cleared up and I could see just what a hole that place was. So I was quite happy when, a few days later, one of the screws came up to me and said, 'Pack your kit, you're being shipped out.'

Wow, I thought, they've finally realised all I've ever done is commit misdemeanours and they're letting me out.

How wrong can you get! It had been decided that Rochester in Kent was the best place for me. In those days, Rochester was a borstal, although it's a D-Category prison now and I've never been back. But back then it was just for kids and it turned out to be a pretty decent place compared with Latchmere. Funnily enough, most cons want to go to Latchmere House now as opposed to Belmarsh or Rochester.

When I got down to Kent, I was put in a holding room with lots of weird characters who seemed to me to be quite mad and talking off the top of their heads about nothing. I thought, Bloody hell, now they've decided to put me in with the nutters.

Then the door opened and in came these guys with trays of fish and chips, and duff and custard. And, as they started handing them out, I thought, That's not enough to feed a rat. The portions of duff – or spotted dick as it's known on the outside – were tiny and the chips looked disgusting.

I spotted one of the kitchen boys pottering about and said, 'Hey, mate, come here.'

Then I whispered to him, 'Four slices of bread, two lumps of that duff and whatever else you can find in the kitchen.'

'OK, mate,' and off he trotted.

A few moments later, the door opened again and I couldn't even see the guy, just the tray, he was so loaded down.

But, as the kitchen hand approached me, some geezer started shouting, 'Hey, man, that's for me, that's for me, man. Not that bloody cripple.'

I have never let, and will never let, anyone call me a cripple. So, as the loudmouth reached for the tray, I got my right crutch and held it up against his neck. The whole place fell silent. I took the tray from the kitchen boy and hissed at the other guy, 'Nobody fucks with my food. Remember that.' Then I set down the tray and began to eat.

That was the first time I made my mark at Rochester and no one dared mess with me after that. I had learned one of the golden rules of prison life – make your mark straight away if you want to survive.

I settled into Rochester quite well. Borstals were working places, and you had to have a job to do. You couldn't just lie in your cell and smoke cannabis, however much you might want to. So they gave me a job on the sewing machines; I was sewing pyjamas and buttons on shirts. I didn't mind that so much. What really got me was having to go back up to London every two weeks for another remand hearing. It meant getting in little green buses and being handcuffed, with your left hand cuffed to the con next to you's right hand. And it used to take ages to get there just to be told by some poxy magistrate that you had to go all the way back to Rochester again.

Such was the routine, though, that it helped me to realise

I had to forget about home, and forget about Chub. I had to forget about even looking forward to going home and I just had to get on with it. That's the best way to do your bird.

Then, one day, I was finally up for sentencing but, because I had already done three months on remand, I was free to go, and so I set off back to Limehouse. But I'd learned a lot in Rochester. I'd learned the crimes you can do and that villains will accept, and the crimes you can't do, like being a nonce or a grass, because even villains will frown at you. If you were a grass or a nonce, your life was not worth living. You'd spend every day looking over your shoulder. I made good friends in that borstal and I stuck up for myself. But I couldn't wait to get home.

As soon as I was released from custody, I made a phone call to Linda.

'I'm out,' I said. 'I'll meet you round Brightlingsea, my place. Bring Chub with you, will you? I've missed him.'

'Duchy, there's something you got to know.'

'Tell me later, Linda, I'm running out of money for the call. I'll see you there in 15 minutes.'

'No, wait, Duchy ...'

But I couldn't. I was on my way home.

When I got there, Linda was already outside. 'I tried to tell you, Duchy, but you wouldn't listen,' she said.

'When did they do this, Linda?'

'About a month ago.'

All the flats at Brightlingsea Buildings had been heavily boarded up prior to them being knocked down. I was homeless again. But I still had my friend and I reached down and stroked good old Chub.

I went down to Social Services but they weren't interested in me, so nothing had changed there. The prison had given me a little bit of money but not enough to survive on. I asked a few friends if I could kip on their sofa but they all came up with excuses and even Linda couldn't help. She wasn't a girlfriend or anything, just a mate, and she had a boyfriend of her own.

There was nothing for it, I'd have to break back into Brightlingsea. And that's what I did. I'd start a fire in one of the grates in a flat to keep myself warm, cover myself with a blanket and go to sleep on the floor next to Chub. Life then was hard, very hard. Next morning, I'd get up and fuck off. That was home for a couple of nights. But it was nothing better than living in a bombed-out old building.

I soon realised I'd have to pop another flat and squat it if I was going to get a decent place to live. That's when I spotted Jamaica House, off the Barley Mow Estate in Limehouse. It was near where the Krays used to hang out in the old days and seemed a fine block of flats to me. So I got a screwdriver, a pair of pliers and some wire, went back to Jamaica House, popped open the door to one of the flats, put the electric on, sorted out the gas and tried to start again. It was a good place and you could see the clocktower and the graveyard opposite The Mission. I was home.

I knew I was all through with nicking cars, although I had to find another way of making money. But in the meantime all I was interested in were some old sticks of furniture and making my home as nice as I could for me and Chub. I had been without a guitar for the three months I had been away, and thought I might have got a bit rusty through lack of practice. But no such thing. I could still rattle off the old songs and so I was soon back down The Five Bells and The Star of the East singing for my supper. If it was a good night, Chub would get a nice piece of meat the next day.

I loved that dog very much, even though he still had a nasty, vicious streak which had been ingrained into him by

Omara. Previously, he had attacked a dog and killed it in the High Street and people started talking about my dog and how bad he was. I had never been able to let him out in the day but now it was worse. We had to sneak out for walks in the middle of the night.

During the time I'd been away in Rochester, Chub had turned even wilder and he would snarl, growl and go to attack people as well as other dogs if he wasn't completely kept in check. He was one real crazy motherfucker, but he was also my friend and we lived together. And that was cool by me.

There was a girl living upstairs from me who also had a badly behaved cross breed named Ricky and she was forced to walk her dog about the same time as me – one or two in the morning – and so we got to know each other. Ricky made even Chub look tame. He was a murderer. He would kill other dogs stone dead.

Even when I was having conversations with this bird in the middle of the night, we had to strain on the dogs' leads to keep them apart.

Then, one day, when I was down in Charlie Brown's, which was really a pub called the Railway Tavern but no one referred to it as that, this guy, whom I'd never seen before, came over to me and introduced himself as Frankie.

'I hear you're the bloke with that dog,' he said.

'What dog?'

'The one that's got a bit of a reputation, that cross Doberman and Alsatian.'

'Yeah, and what's it to you?'

'Would you like to make some money?'

'And?'

'Well, I could fix him up, your dog against mine.'

I knew it wasn't a good idea but something was telling me, 'Do it, do it,' and teach this guy a lesson.

I tried to stay cool. 'What kind of dog you got?' I said.
'Staff.'

I almost choked. A Staffordshire Bull Terrier. They were a top breed of fighting dog. I still had time to back out. I hadn't committed either me or Chub to anything.

But instead I said, 'OK,' and tried to look nonchalant.

Dog fighting has been illegal in Britain since 1835 but has always been there, underground. The best breeds for fighting are Staffs and American Pit Bull Terriers and, of course, Rottweilers know how to handle themselves. But I didn't know anything about this when Frankie happened upon me. All I knew was that, if Chub won, I'd get £300, which to me was a fortune at the time.

Dog fighting is a gambling sport in which large bets are often placed on the outcome of each fight. And good dogs can change hands for more than a grand a time. The dogs are brutally trained to develop a taste for blood and flesh and then subjected to exhausting exercise, often using treadmills, to improve their muscle strength.

I just thought if I exercised Chub a bit more before it came to the big day then that would probably be all right. That's how naïve I was.

One evening only a few days before the fight, there was a knock on my door and I was totally dumbstruck when I opened it. Standing in the hallway of the flats were my mum and dad, the Reverend and Mrs Jeff Peter.

'Hello, son, I've been worried about you,' said Mum.

I hadn't had any contact with my parents since they had tried to persuade me to go back to their house in Forest Hill after I'd been thrown out of Nottingham Technical College. I had resisted them then. Now what did they want?

They had automatically been informed about me being sent down to borstal and they had kept in touch with my after-care social worker. He must have told them where I was squatting. When I was in Rochester, Mum and Dad had wanted to visit me, but I turned down all requests. I wouldn't let them visit me in prison.

I had been brought up by the Rodriguez family in the belief that, if you get yourself into trouble, you get yourself out. You don't go running to anyone else. I also held the view that it was disrespectful for the police to go to my parents' house and search it for things which concerned me. And I would never want to see my mum stroll up to a prison gate to visit me. And anyway, why had they put me into care as soon as I was born? And what did they want now?

All the fear and all the unanswered questions instilled in me by the very idea of my father came flooding back. But, at the same time, I felt a sense of pride as he looked around the flat, eyeing things up. I'd managed to get a bit of carpet down and got myself an old three-piece suite. It wasn't a mansion and it was nothing like their house in Forest Hill, but it was my home and there was a fierce determination in my steely gaze as my father said to me in those measured tones of his, 'I can see you have made up your mind, Raymond.'

He looked around the room again slowly and nodded imperceptibly. 'You have your friends and your flat and I can't take any of this from you.'

I just stared straight ahead.

'But, if you wish to come home, you may come home,' he added.

At this point, Mum started to cry, and seeing her like that I started to well up too.

'But, if you do come home, you come home under my rules and my laws,' finished Dad.

I held my quivering lip still and looked my dad straight in the eye. What I wanted was an answer to the age-old question – why had this God-fearing man of the cloth have me put into a home? But I was no nearer to getting that answer, so, with as much dignity as I could muster, I simply said, 'I'm fine here, thank you, Dad. Why don't you take Mum home … I think it's upsetting her.'

And, with that, I opened the door for them. I missed my mum so much. I thought I would never see them again but back then I just had to have them a million miles away from me.

With only a couple of days to the dog fight, I tried to put my parents' visit out of my mind, but I couldn't shake that image of my mum sitting there on my battered old armchair, tears rolling down her cheeks.

* * *

Dog fights nearly always take place at night in outbuildings, barns, lock-ups or derelict premises, anywhere that's hidden from public view. Frankie had organised it in another squat just downstairs from my flat in Jamaica House. The fighting pit or 'box' is a makeshift ring and marked in half across the middle with a 'scratch-line'. Frankie had decided to set up the box in the large kitchen of the deserted flat with the box itself enclosed by boards about 2ft high.

By the time I arrived with Chub, there were already quite a few dog-fight fanciers there and lots of cash bets going on, many of them running into hundreds of pounds.

I had never seen anything like it before; there was electricity in the air. Frankie's Staff looked like it had been in two or three riots. The dog was scarred all over with part of its ear missing and looked like the meanest dog on earth. The punters standing round the box also looked like some of the most brutal people you'd ever meet in London's East

End and that's saying something. There was only one lightbulb in the whole place and that was above the box sending garish light and dark shadows everywhere. It looked like a scene from hell and I remember thinking, I don't want to do this, I don't want to do this any more. But then I looked up and there was this guy Frankie with a smirk on his face.

An old dog-fight fan took me to one side and said, 'How much you getting for the beefing, son?'

'The what? I don't know what you're talking about.'

'Keep it to yourself then. But I know Frankie's dog needs a good beefing before he takes it down Mile End.'

'No, I'm just here for a … for a … fight,' I suddenly started to stammer, realising I was into something way over my head and there was no turning back.

Later, I learned that Frankie had been looking for a 'beef' for his Staff – a trial fight usually involving the killing of an inferior dog before the main fight. Most top fighting dogs are 'beefed-up' like this before they go into a big major fight. Once they have made the kill and tasted blood, they are at the peak of their fighting prowess for a few days. Stolen pets, dogs and sometimes cats, are used as training material for top dogs and for beefing them up before a major fight. But, rather than letting me know and giving me a bit of money, Frankie clearly preferred to see my dog rolled-out and killed for nothing.

I had walked into this whole thing with my eyes closed just because I was greedy for £300. Frankie's dog had probably killed half the dogs in the neighbourhood for all I knew. I didn't stand a chance and I wasn't even getting a kickback in beefing money.

Worst of all, there was no backing out. I couldn't back out because people had been placing bets. If Frankie's dog wasn't given a chance to kill Chub, then the spectators would more than likely kill me. So I just had to go along with it and, before I knew it, the dogs were in the ring.

You have to take off all chains, collars and anything else the dog may have on and put him into the box, holding him back by a cloth or a piece of leather around his neck. Then you get the dogs to face each other while you restrain them. As the dogs face each other, you bait them with shouts of encouragement, as do the crowd, and the temper of the dogs starts to rise.

The dogs are then turned away from each other as the crowd keeps hollering; then you get the dogs to face each other again, and again you gee up the dogs and taunt them. On the third face, when fever pitch has been reached, the referee says, 'Gentlemen, release your dogs.' And the fight begins.

The Bull Terrier charged at Chub going straight for his throat and trying to rip it out. But he missed and the two dogs locked their massive jaws together, shaking each other wildly as cuts formed around their mouths and the blood mixed with their saliva. As the dogs shook their heads together, the blood and saliva started splashing over the crowd outside the box. The spectators were in a frenzy with shouts of 'Seize him … Shake him … Kill the bastard.'

The Staff pulled back over the scratch-line then lunged again as powerfully as possible, with all his defined muscles taut and straining, at Chub who looked dazed from the first encounter. This time he went for Chub's neck. But being a long-haired cross helped save him. Instead of a mouthful of flesh, all the Staff got was a load of fur. He couldn't grip on to the dog.

I glanced over at Frankie. The smirk had disappeared from his face.

The old punter, who thought I was there for a beefing, leaned over to me and said, 'Why do you call your dog Chub?'

I didn't know. That was his name when I bought him from Omara. But quick as a flash I replied, Cos he locks on hard.'

And that's just what he did. With the Staff's mouth full of fur, Chub pounced and sank his teeth into the dog's smooth-skinned neck. Blood was everywhere. Then, as quick as lightning, Chub released his grip and bit straight into the bottom of the Staff's ear. The crowd roared.

It was Frankie's turn to look over at me. He was serious now.

Growling and fighting mad, the Staff fought back until both dogs had their jaws locked again and it looked like they were each trying to rip the other's head off. It was as much a test of wills as it was of strength.

After the first wild attacks, the fight settled into a pattern of locking jaws, scrambling, shaking and locking jaws again; each dog trying to wear down the strength of the other so they could go for a kill.

There are no rounds or anything like that in dog fighting and many fights go on for more than an hour. And you can't pull your dog out and throw the towel in unless the dog looks like it's about to be killed. If the fight looks even, then it's all down to the referee. But in many mismatched bouts the underdog can be killed in a matter of minutes even before the referee can take action. That's what Frankie had been banking on, but he had got it wrong.

After another ten or 15 minutes I could sense Chub was starting to run out of steam. He was covered in blood and slowing up while the Staff was still tensing his muscles and baring his teeth. But, every time he tried to get a grip on Chub's flesh, once again he slipped off with only a mouthful of hair. And this was making the Staff angry, it wasn't something he was used to. And that anger made him hesitate. It was just enough hesitation for Chub to switch tactics from locking jaws to burying his teeth into the Staff's neck. An almighty howl went up and something happened that no one ever thought they would see. The Staff turned away from Chub.

Whenever a dog turns away in a fight, the referee has the right to call the fight off for 15 seconds, which is exactly what he did.

I grabbed Chub, who was slippery with blood and saliva, and held him back with the restraining cloth.

The crowd, who were so vociferous earlier, were now stunned into silence. Everyone held their breath as the referee gave the Staff a mandatory 15 seconds to cross the scratch-line and bite, or 'mouth' as it's known, Chub while he was being held back.

It was the longest 15 seconds of my life. I could sense everyone in that kitchen counting to themselves as the referee looked at his stopwatch.

Nine ... ten ... eleven ... the Staff was crossing the scratch-line! My heart sank ... 12 ... 13 ... I held Chub tightly, determined to let him fly on 15. Only two seconds remaining, one second and then ... the Staff slowly rolled over and offered his throat and belly to Chub.

We had won.

Pandemonium broke out. Both dogs were taken out of the box and I put my arms around Chub not caring about the filth and the blood.

Frankie stepped over to me, trying to muster as broad a smile as he could. 'Your dog did well,' he said as he shook my hand. 'That's the first time mine's been beaten. Here's your £300.'

'Thanks,' I quietly replied, pocketing the cash while fixing Chub's muzzle and collar. 'I hope yours recovers well ...' and I turned to go.

'Before you're off,' he said. 'Do you fancy a return match soon?'

I thought he was a bit of a glutton for punishment, but said nothing.

'Your Chub up against two Staffs, for £600.'

I swallowed hard. 'I'll think about it,' I mumbled, and headed for the door.

A few days later, I was sitting in Charlie Brown's when in walked Linda with her latest boyfriend, an Italian chap named Serge, I think and we got talking. Linda had always been interested in Chub ever since she looked after him while I was in borstal. Now she knew he was a good fighter she wanted him.

'I get you Neapolitan mastiff in change for Chub,' said Serge. 'Nice Neapolitan mastiff. Very good dog.'

'Nah thanks, I'm happy with him.'

'But Neapolitan mastiff is very good, Duchy, very brutal dog.'

'Leave it out, Serge.'

Every time I bumped into Serge, he would go on about this bloody Italian dog, but my mind was elsewhere. I was toying with the idea of £600 for Chub beating two Staffs.

One night, out walking Chub, I spotted the girl upstairs who was exercising Ricky.

'I've been offered £600 for Chub versus two Staffs ... whaddya think?' I asked her.

'You're raving mad, Duchy. The dog will be killed, you won't get your £600 and, anyway, Chub is supposed to be a pet.'

'Yeah, but it's a lot of money.'

And it was the money that changed my mind.

The next time I bumped into Frankie, which was about six weeks later, I said, 'You still up for Chub and your Staffs?' Of course he was; a date was agreed on and the box was going to be set up in a different place. It is policy never to use the same place twice when you're dog fighting, in case the police get wind of it.

After seeing his first fight, I honestly thought that Chub could take on two dogs and win, but at the same time I was reluctant to put my theory to the test.

But the night of the fight came and I had learned a lot about training Chub since his last ordeal. He was in better shape than ever. He was leaner and more fierce.

Frankie put in his original Staff first and we faced off the dogs and baited them as usual.

Chub was tougher now, and whether or not he recognised he was up against the Staff he had fought so valiantly only a few weeks earlier I don't know, but he took the fight to him straight away. He beat the dog even more convincingly this time and Frankie went mad. He started shouting and screaming. He didn't want the fight stopped this time until he had won, and so he threw the second fresh Staff into the ring in a desperate bid to see off Chub.

But Chub, bloodied from his first battle, took on the second Staff as well. It was a grisly, awful, appalling fight but it's a sight I will never forget. Bashed, battered and bruised, Chub hung in there and stood up to the gnarled old Staff until, after what seemed like a whole night of fighting, the referee declared my dog the winner.

Chub and I went to hell and back that night but when I had the £600 in my pocket and Chub in my arms I whispered into his ear, 'Never again, old mate ... I'll never allow this to happen again.'

But with two major fights under his belt Chub's notoriety began to spread and I started getting invited down to Mile End, then the Mecca for dog-fighting in London's East End. Down there anything went in the dog fighting game. They even used to have fights in what were little more than beefing-up vans. Someone would get a blacked-out old Post Office van or something similar and they were open for business.

I remember being horrified when I saw one of these vans. 'What's all this about?' I asked a mate of mine who had taken me down there. I was genuinely puzzled. The van wasn't big enough for spectators to get in and barely big enough to hold a conventional box.

'It's extreme dog fighting,' I was told.

'How's it work?'

'Well, in there is a bloody great Rottweiler.'

'And?'

'Well, look, you'll see. It's about to start.'

There was a lot of money changing hands around the van, and a lot of calculations being done. This wasn't like any dog fighting I'd seen before. Then, when the betting was finished, the referee, if he can be called that, said, 'Right, open the door.' With that, the door was opened and, as fast as lightning, this Pit Bull Terrier was thrown in and the door closed as quickly as possible.

The sounds coming from inside the van were terrifying. It seemed to be like a prolonged howling, growling and screeching.

In less than five or ten minutes, the door of the van was opened again and this time the dead body of the English Bull Terrier was hauled out and thrown on the ground.

Next up was another dog and the whole process of betting and calculating started again.

You could bet on which dog would survive or which one would be killed, taking into account the Rottweiler was getting weaker each time it fought; how many fights the Rottweiler might survive; all sorts of bets. It was pure slaughter and far too barbaric for me because I didn't want to see Chub killed, no matter how much I could win.

That's when Frankie made a very tempting offer.

'Duchy, my boy,' he said. 'How about £1,000 guaranteed to you whatever the outcome of the fight to put Chub up against that other ... what's-its-name ... mongrel you're always hanging around with?'

'Ricky,' I said astonished.

'Yeah, that's it, Ricky. A grand for you if you can get them both in the ring. The punters are getting a bit fed up with these fighting breeds and want to see a bit more sport. How about it?'

'No way,' I said emphatically, while working out how I'd broach the subject with the girl upstairs.

'You're having a laugh, ain't you, Duch?' she said, when I told her. 'There's no way I'm going to have my Ricky fighting in a ring.'

'But it's a grand. We could split the money.'

'But, Duchy,' she said, her voice rising in pitch, 'we'd be fucking up two dogs, and yours has already taken enough of a beating for a lifetime.'

So she refused to do it and I had to tell Frankie the fight wasn't on, not now, not ever.

I was drowning my sorrows in Charlie Brown's thinking what I could have done with that grand, when Serge comes up to me.

'You want Neapolitan mastiff now, you have to pay,' he said. 'Linda, she no longer wanta your dog. Your dog now too scarred.'

'Well, fuck her,' I said. 'I don'
anyway.'

'OK, Duchy, OK.'

And as we talked, Serg
going to a better place. So
collecting up his bits and pieces a.
down to East India Dock Road in Popla.
lived. I'd never liked the area since I'd had
with a bloke down there a few weeks earlier.
threatened to stab me over something so trivial I can't ev
remember what it was, but I did brag to him at the time,
'Bring it on, boy. Don't threaten my life because I will kill
you in the street, there's no doubt about that.'

But this night, fortunately, things seemed very quiet.
Trent had managed to get hold of a small old van to carry
his stuff away in. I must say it was one of the best
furnished squats I had ever seen. It must have been the
Italian in him.

'Why on earth are you leaving a lovely squat like this,
Serge?' I asked.

'Oh, is not mine, is a friend of mine. I have been staying
here. Now I have place of my own and need to move my
stuff out.'

We gathered up loads of bits and pieces, some paintings,
a few lamps, nothing too big.

'Furniture and stuff belong to my friend,' explained Serge.

I took a shine to a lovely ashtray with a view of Rome on
it. 'That's nice, Serge, did you bring it from Italy?'

'You keep it, Duchy, for helping me out tonight.'

'Cheers, mate.'

We loaded everything into the van. I stuck the ashtray in
my pocket and off I went down to Linda's.

Later that night, after I got home, I decided to take Chub

ghtly walk. I let him off his lead, 'cos there was no
e around, and he disappeared. I lit up my joint, and
ed around, turning over this ashtray in my pocket,
thinking there was always something not quite right
out Serge.

But I put it to the back of my mind because coming towards
me was the guy I'd had a barney with down the East India
Dock Road a couple of weeks before. He was running straight
at me and he had a bloody great big knife in his hand.

I wasn't tooled up, but I had my crutches and I stood my
ground. With the area barely lit by the stars and the moon,
disarming him in such bad light would depend on whether
my reactions would be fast enough. I put one crutch back,
my artificial legs forward for balance and swung the right
crutch. But I missed the knife! And, although the blow
to his arm made my assailant stumble, he continued to
lunge at me from only 4ft away and looked certain to
strike home. With the knife only inches from connecting,
there was an almighty growl as Chub sprang out of the
shadows and pounced on the guy's back, knocking him to
the ground.

I quickly picked up the knife as Chub continued to tear
and shred at the geezer's clothes, looking to sink his teeth
into warm flesh.

'Call off the dog … call off the fucking dog,' he shouted,
trying to cover his head with his arms.

'I warned you,' I said softly to him while Chub continued
to growl and shake his victim. And with that I brought
down the crutch as hard as I could, cracking open the
geezer's head.

'Heel, Chub, there's a good dog,' I said as I rolled the guy
over with my artificial legs and kicked him as hard as I could
in the balls. 'And as for you … don't ever let me see you

round here again.' With that, I put the leash on Chub. 'Come on,' I said, 'we're going home. You're a guard dog now. There'll be no more fighting for you.'

Clat … clat … clat … clat …

The Old Bill came round about a week later. They had arrested Serge and he coughed the lot; he even dragged me into it. It transpired the 'mate's squat' he had been moving out of that night was, in fact, a flat that belonged to an old lady who was in hospital.

Once they spotted the ashtray, the questioning began. I told them I hadn't had anything to do with the burglary and I thought I was just giving a mate a helping hand to move.

'That's the best one we've heard yet, Duchy. You're coming down the station, mate, you're nicked.'

I didn't stand a chance. I was still on probation from previous misdemeanours so with my latest 'Burglary and Theft – Dwelling', I knew I'd be remanded in custody again.

What I didn't know was where I would be going. Because the system wasn't really made to cope with disabled people, instead of being sent to a borstal again I was sent to an adult prison – Lewes, a Victorian building in East Sussex dating back to the 1850s, which housed some of the hardest bastards in the country.

What the fuck was going to become of me in a place like that?

6

System Addict

THERE WERE FOUR or five of us in the sweat box; each in our own tiny cell as the driver put the big white van into gear and moved out from the back of the magistrates' court. The small blacked-out windows didn't let anyone look in, and we didn't want to look out. We all knew where we were going, because sweat boxes like ours headed there from all over the capital – Lambeth in South London, a holding nick where they kept you while they allocated you to a permanent prison.

When we got out we were lined up in front of the desk sergeant. 'Peter KF 3675. Go over there, you're up for remand again in two weeks.'

Clat … clat … clat … clat … I moved over into another room which was full of cons waiting to hear their fate. What a bunch they were. It didn't matter whether they were standing, sitting or lounging about, they all had that look of insolence on their faces. I thought, Jesus Christ, what the fuck's going on here? I'd never seen so many hardened-looking geezers in one place before. Some of them I recognised.

'Hello, Charlie, long time, mate. Billy boy! How's the old lady? Bloody hell, it's Peter the Pipe, innit?'

And some of them came up to me. 'Duchy, how's it going?'

While a few of us were getting to know each other again, a screw came over to me and said, 'Right, we've got to have those crutches.'

'Not having them,' I said, as everyone stopped talking to see what would happen next.

But the screw just snatched them off me while I stared at him with hate in my eyes.

But he didn't blink. 'And those fucking tin legs as well, get them off,' he ordered.

'I'll need to sit down.'

So he brought me a wheelchair. And all the time I stared at him and all he could see was pure venom in my face.

Then he cracked. 'Listen,' he said. 'That's the rules, I'm just following orders. Crutches ain't allowed, or prostheses, just in case they might be used as weapons. Now come on, be a good lad.' And with that he helped me into the wheelchair.

The noise level in the room started to rise again and I sat there for what seemed like hours. Then this bloke came out of the toilet, which was off the room, and whispered to a geezer standing near me, 'Come on, I think I found something. The bloody ceiling in the toilet's hollow.'

And there he was, standing on top of the lavatory, tapping at the ceiling. And sure enough, it sounded like thin plasterboard. We all looked at each other and the same thought flashed through everyone's mind at the same time – escape.

The idea was to try and bash a hole in the ceiling and see where it led. But there was one small problem – we didn't have anything to make the hole with.

'Hey, mate,' said the guy who had discovered the plasterboard ceiling. 'Come over here and get out of your wheelchair, we'll use that.'

So I jumped out of the wheelchair and sat on the floor. By this time, I was nimble even when I didn't have my legs on and I could walk perfectly on my hands. In fact, woe betide anyone who thought they could take advantage of me in that situation. They'd have to think again.

So the wheelchair was collapsed and folded up and the guys took it into the toilet. They hoisted it above their heads and started using it as a battering ram. Bang … bang … it went into the ceiling while some blokes kept a look-out for the screws and the majority of cons acted normally with their voices raised a bit to try and cover the banging.

The plasterboard was easily broken through and all this dirt and shit was everywhere but there was a hole in the ceiling, that's all that mattered, and finally they made an area big enough for a human being to get through.

The bloke who'd originated the 'escape attempt' decided to go first but, as soon as he got his head into the hole in the ceiling, he realised it was never going to be big enough.

'There's only a small amount of space, very fucking little indeed, between the ceiling and the floor upstairs,' he whispered down to us. 'It's not big enough for a grown man to crawl through.'

Then he pointed at me. 'Hey, you, you with no legs, you're small enough. Come and have a go.'

With that, two of them grabbed me and lifted me up to the hole. I valiantly tried to hoist myself into the space but even I couldn't get in. It was only about 18 inches high.

So there I was, half-in and half-out, when I heard this voice – 'KF 3675 Peter.'

Christ, the screws were calling me. 'That's me,' I said looking down at my new mates. Everything seemed to freeze for a millisecond and then there was pandemonium. Two guys pulled me out of the hole in the ceiling, while another put up the wheelchair and then they threw me into it and pushed it into the main room just as the door opened and there was another shout of, 'KF 3675 Peter,' from the desk sergeant.

'Oh, there you are ...' he started as a look of amazement came over his face. Covered in dust and plaster, I resembled someone from the *Black and White Minstrel Show*.

Immediately, he twigged something was going on and the alarm bell went off, alerting the Old Bill to secure the building.

I just sat there in my wheelchair with a sly smile on my face as the cogs turned in the sergeant's mind. Surely it couldn't be possible ... the guy's in a wheelchair and has no legs, he was thinking.

Then he put his face close up to mine and snarled, 'Peter, if you've been up to what I think you have, then I'm going to do you for absconding.'

I just looked at him, held out my hands, shrugged and said, 'I ain't been anywhere and I ain't going anywhere. How could I go anywhere? I'm a disabled man and you've confiscated my legs and my crutches.'

He grew visibly redder as the anger rose in his voice.

'Well, you're going somewhere now,' he said. 'You going to Lewes Prison in East Sussex. And God help you if you try to come the clever dick there. You can pick your crutches up at the desk.' And with that he turned around smartly and left.

* * *

Lewes was an old Victorian prison built in the 1850s on a hill. It was like a big old castle, like being captured by the Black Baron and slung into one of his dungeons. Because it was on a hill, the higher you went up the hill, the colder it got. And there were no real heaters in there in those days. It was freezing cold all the time, except in the summer when some tiny heating pipes were put on. That's how perverse things were at Lewes with its six wings from A to F and its massive overcrowding, slopping out and 23-hour bang-ups. We had no toilets so we had to use shit-pots, which we emptied every morning. It was a powder keg of madness.

I was really apprehensive about going to Lewes. It was another part of the same system that started with the Social Services moving me around from one children's home to another. Now, because of my disability, I was being shoved into any nick that had space for a cripple. The prison system wasn't designed to cope with disabled people so I had to go wherever there was a bit of room. Years later, I would be left in the notorious Thamesmead nick, Belmarsh, because other prisons refused to take me, even though Belmarsh was only supposed to be an allocation nick. What if he has an accident? Where's he going to work? He can't lift paving slabs. Leave him in Belmarsh. Leave him where he is. Leave him to rot.

So I was feeling down as we approached the Black Baron's castle, but things took a decided turn for the better when I saw who I was sharing a cell with.

'Mark, bloody Mark Richardson,' I exclaimed as soon as the cell door banged shut.

'Duch. Fucking hell, Duch, what you doing here?'

'I could ask you the same.'

Mark had been a rockabilly mate of mine when we used to hang out in Lewisham Shopping Precinct as young teenagers. Maybe it wasn't going to be so bad after all. We swapped a few details. Mark was in for fighting; I should have guessed that. Mark was the best fighter I'd ever known. And then we got down to reminiscing about the great times we'd had round the Puppet Café and all the scrapes we used to get into. And how we used to hang out at the Squire pub which had a club on the side of it called Chickabooms.

'Remember that time you got hung up looking at some skateboards?' he said.

'I used to have one of them,' I replied.

We laughed.

'Remember the time you had that fight outside The Swan and Sugarloaf in Croydon?' said Mark.

'How could I forget! The guy tried to strangle me from behind, and had my teeth marks in his armpit for a week.'

We laughed.

'My dad's in here as well,' said Mark. 'So we should be all right.'

'Why's that?' I asked stupidly.

''Cos he's my dad.'

I looked more perplexed. And suddenly Mark burst out laughing again. 'You mean you never knew, Duch? You never sussed,' he said incredulously.

'Knew fucking what? What you going on about?'

'My dad,' laughed Mark. 'My dad's Charlie ... Charlie Richardson.'

'Yeah, all right,' I said sarcastically, 'and I'm Metal Mickey.'

But he was telling the truth. All those years and I never knew one of my best mates was the son of one of Britain's most notorious criminals. Charlie and his brother Edward were almost as famous as the Krays. But they were never convicted of murder like Ronnie and Reggie. Instead, the police insisted their game was torture and extortion, although Charlie has always maintained it was a frame-up. When they were finally nicked, Charlie got 25 years and here he was in Lewes. Well, what do you know?

Also banged up in our cell was a Hell's Angel biker, one of the nastiest motherfuckers I'd ever seen in my life. He had a shaved and tattooed head – in fact, he was tattooed just about everywhere – and had this permanent sneer on his face. He was in there for four years and, instead of getting on with his bird, he hated every minute of it. He looked like he was going to explode at any moment.

He used to say to me, 'I really like you, Duch ... trouble is, I can't stand niggers.'

I tried to keep myself to myself. Apart from Mark, there was a little firm of black guys there run by a bloke named Syd whom I also knew from outside. And we used to hang around together the one hour a day we weren't banged up. Every couple of weeks, I'd go back up to London to get remanded and then sent back to Lewes.

Although the system was getting to me – remember, my life had been one of institutions – I wasn't frightened of anyone in those days. I could handle myself many times better than able-bodied people and I was fearless when it came to fighting. I went into Lewes thinking, OK, let's make the best of it and get on with it.

But I got tired of hearing about some young guys getting bullied all the time by this bloke named Pillar who was a bit of a face in the East End, mainly because his family had a reputation.

I was in the exercise yard one day watching some lads running round. Most of them were like shit and falling all over the place except for this strong kid who was out in front. He was showing off and shouting to the others, 'You're all fucking useless. Next one I overtake will fucking get it.'

'Who's that guy?' I asked Mark.

'That's Pillar, Duch. That's Paul.'

So, as a joke, I shouted at him, 'Don't slow down, mate, don't slow down.' And he didn't think that was very funny at all.

Next thing I know, he stops running and walks over to Mark and me.

'Who the fuck do you think you are?' he starts.

I just looked at him. 'I don't have to think,' I said. 'I know who I am.'

'You sound like a smart cunt to me.'

But, as he tried to take the piss and belittle me, I suddenly realised that, while everyone else was scared of Paul, I wasn't going to be intimidated.

He gave it a little bit of verbal for a while and then said, 'Don't think because you're a cripple I won't knock you out.'

'Don't let anything stop you, mate,' I replied, staring him straight in the eyes. 'Bring it on, bring it fucking well on.'

He had threatened me and I had threatened him. Everyone knew there had to be a confrontation to sort things out, but just at that moment a couple of screws arrived out of nowhere, separated us and took us away. I glanced back and could see Paul was as angry as fuck.

It was decided through notes and one thing and another that me and Paul would meet at dinner-time and sort it out and have a fight.

Everyone in the nick heard about it and thought there was going to be an off that dinner-time.

'Are you sure, Duch? You could back down,' said Mark when we were back in the cell.

'Fuck off, Mark. That's funny coming from you. You're one of the best fighters I've ever known. You don't back down and neither do I. That geezer's got to be pulled down a peg or two. He's bullying all the little boys in here who wouldn't say fucking boo to a goose, but that's Paul. None of the bastards I know would want to be seen fighting a cripple. If you fuck with someone like me you deserve everything you get.'

'Well, I'll be watching your back,' said the biker, who showed me what looked like the heavy metal shank of a dart. 'I'll hit him straight in the eye with this if he tries any funny business. I'm watching your back, mate.'

That's when I realised the biker really did like me.

Mark only had a pencil, but he said, 'And I'll stab him with this.'

Syd and his firm were talking about it, everybody seemed to know there was going to be an off. And I suppose that's why, when dinner-time came round, neither me nor Pillar were allowed out of our cells.

'You'll stay in here, Peter, this dinner,' said one of the screws.

'Why's that?'

''Cos I say so.'

Minutes later, the cell door opened again and in stepped the PO (Principal Officer), a big bloke whom you never saw very often unless you were in the shit. He had ginger hair, ginger glasses, a ginger beard and huge arms like tree trunks. Everybody feared him, but I thought he was OK.

'Peter,' he said. 'I hear you have a problem.'

'No problem.'

'Not what I hear. That's why we are keeping you here. Then we are going to let you get your food on your own. Then we are going to let that other scumbag pal of yours Paul get his food on his own. Have I made myself clear?'

I just looked straight ahead.

'And if you think you are going to patch up your differences in this prison you're wrong. I don't want it, and the Governor doesn't want it. Understand?'

I continued staring straight ahead. We both knew who would win.

'Don't push it. I'm itching for an excuse to take you down the block,' he said as he turned and left.

'Then let him out, let him out with me,' I shouted as the cell door banged shut.

That night, Mark got out a bit of puff so we could all have a smoke in the cell.

'Where did you get that?' I asked.

'Dad sent it down. And he says, "Tell Duch I think he did proud standing up to that bully. Have a smoke on me."'

'Where does he get it from?'

'From the bleeding screws, stupid. Now shut up and roll one.'

I never saw Paul again inside. I don't know where they spirited him to but he was never out on the exercise yard when I was and he was never having dinner when I was. I think they must have shipped him out. Well, maybe not them, but I think Charlie might have shipped him out.

But I was never allowed to forget the incident. You are never allowed to forget anything in the nick because at night there was a constant barrage of yelling and shouting and piss-taking from one cell to another.

On and on it would go, an all-night barrage. And it wasn't just me, everybody would get it, about everything. It was constant shouting from the stir-crazy and the just plain mental. The only time I could ever get any of them to quiet down was when I sang. I wasn't allowed a guitar in the nick but I had a good voice and could sing unaccompanied. Someone would shout, 'Sing us to sleep, Duchy.' Then they'd all burst out laughing and screaming again.

But, when they did quieten down, I'd do requests. One favourite was Procol Harum's 'A Whiter Shade of Pale'.

Even the screws used to ask me to sing. 'You'll be famous,' they'd say. 'You're a bloody good singer, you.'

The yelling and shouting was a nightly occurrence, as it is in all prisons. The screws couldn't stop it, nobody could. There would be shouts of, 'Oi, Duchy, I'm going to get you.' And the next day I'd go and try to find out who was doing all the shouting. And I got the same answer all the time – 'It wasn't me, Duch, it was him.'

But one day, a message came over from F-Wing. 'Charlie Richardson says he has to get up at 5.00am tomorrow morning. If one con is caught shouting out of those windows, you'll be weighed in.'

And you know what? That night there was not a dicky bird, not a sound at all. It was eerie. I had never known anything like that before and I don't think anyone else had either.

Now that, to me, was a sign of power. Charlie was the daddy of the prison, there was no doubt about that.

In the small exercise yard, you just walked round and round like something out of *One Flew Over the Cuckoo's Nest*, and I decided that wasn't for me. Instead, I opted to use the gymnasium because, ever since the days on the roof at Prince's Lodge, I'd kept myself in shape. My upper body strength was pretty awesome because of my disability and I didn't want to lose it by being banged up 23 hours a day. So I decided to work out.

The first person I met there was an old bodybuilding mate of mine, Eric, who used to work with me on the door at a pub in the East End. When I wasn't singing my songs in the pub, I used to double up as a bouncer.

'Bloody hell,' I said, 'Eric! It seems everybody I know's in here.'

'Duch, mate. How's it going?'

Eric was the gym orderly because of his size and strength. He had been a diamond bloke at the White Swan, which often had its fair share of trouble. I remember once this mature couple in the pub were always getting drunk and a bit too amorous. Many times I had to ask them to leave because they were upsetting the customers. One night, going back to my squat, I heard this commotion round the side of the pub and, when I went to investigate, I saw this same old lady but she had been glassed by a young girl from the pub. It was absolutely shocking. But that's the kind of place the pub was and that's why they needed people like me and Eric to try and calm things down.

While I was doing me press-ups and Eric was making sure the gym was all in order, I asked one of the questions you rarely ask in the nick unless you know the con pretty well.

'What you in for, Eric?' I said.

'Murder,' he replied dryly.

I couldn't imagine it. He was a big bruiser and very muscular. But he was more of a gentle giant than anything else.

We started talking. 'It was all the usual stuff, Duch,' he said. 'You know how it was down there.'

And I did. The White Swan wasn't the roughest or even the toughest boozer in the East End, but it attracted geezers who, when they've had a few, thought they could take on the world. And, because of my mate's size, they were always taunting him with, 'You think you're hard, don't you? Well, come on then, let's see how hard you are.'

I'm amazed he kept his cool for as long as he did under those circumstances. But one day I guess he just lost it.

'One night, this bloke just kept going on and on, Duch. He was drunk and mouthing off,' said Eric. 'So I thought I'll just take him outside and give him a little slap, teach him a bit of a lesson. His attitude was putting off other customers wanting to get into the pub.

'Anyway, we went outside and he was still giving it plenty of mouth. I warned him I might have to hit him if he didn't stop. And that's exactly what I did. But that one punch killed him, Duch. And now I'm banged up in here. Make sure it don't happen to you, Duch.'

I was starting to fear the system, a system that had begun when I was in children's homes and in which I was still caught up. And so I rebelled – big time. I wasn't going to be marooned or bullied into anything, not by the screws, not by anyone.

When the screws started to get a bit handy with me, I started to get a bit handy with them. And, just like the times when I would fight the police, I was now fighting the prison officers. Frankly, I didn't conform. But I was more worried about them giving me the 'liquid cosh', Largactil, than anything else they could do to me.

In Lewes, they would liquid cosh anyone they thought might be even the slightest threat to their law and order.

Largactil is used to treat serious mental and emotional disorders, including schizophrenia and other psychotic illnesses. In Lewes, it was used to keep everyone quiet. Back then, you never saw a black man in the mental health unit, but nowadays the nicks are full of 'em.

I never got the liquid cosh, but I did get sent to the 'block', which is an isolation cell. Although not quite padded, it had everything made out of cardboard so you can't use anything as a weapon. The first time I was sent to the block was when I had a fight with a kid in the gymnasium over something trivial. He thought he had given me a pasting in the gym but, by the time we got back to the changing room, I had my own opinion and I clubbed him viciously with a big Ever Ready battery.

It was while in the block that I realised the place was full of loonies. Everyone seemed to be on Largactil.

An immense fear overwhelmed me at the time. I didn't think I would ever get out of Lewes, that I would be forgotten and just left there forever.

Mark used to say, 'Come on, you'll be all right. Remember the rockabilly days when we did this and that, remember the good days and focus on that.'

But I was being drained by the number of times I was being dragged back and forth to the block. I hated the block so much I used to sit by my door and shout, 'Remember that screw that hit me? Well, I ain't forgotten and as soon as you open this door I am going to wound one of you because of what he did to me.'

That's the way it was. One of them hit me, and I hit any one of them. It didn't matter who it was.

The screws were terrified of me and used to shout, 'Stand well away from the door … we are bringing your food in.'

Eventually, I started to calm down and was let back into a normal cell. But instead of being back with my old mate Mark Richardson and the biker geezer, I was put in with another black guy.

I thought, Hello, here we go again. Just like in the children's homes, they obviously think it better to keep blacks with blacks.

I didn't recognise the guy at first because he was sat all huddled up in the corner of the cell. But, as I looked closer, I thought, I'm sure I know him.

'Tony?' I said quietly. 'Is that you, Tony?'

I knew Tony from the Lewisham days. He used to be one of Syd's little crew. He was a top man, well dressed and well loved by the women. Yeah, Tony used to be top money. But I could hardly recognise him now. He had an empty look in his eyes and was just sitting there rocking back and forth a little.

'Tony,' I repeated as I gently shook his shoulder, 'is that you? It's Duch here, remember me?'

Then he slowly looked up, his eyes totally glazed and said, 'Duch, I hear you, man. I hear what you are saying.'

I didn't know what had happened to Tony but it frightened me. He had turned into a total vegetable and I was determined I was not going to go that way.

Before they threw me in the cell with Tony, the screws took away my crutches.

I banged on the closed door. 'Hey, hey, hey,' I shouted.

The small window in the door opened. 'What do you want?'

'I want my fucking crutches.'

'Can't have 'em.'

'Why not?'

'Because you're banged up with a loony. He's as nutty as a fruit cake and, as much as we would like to see it, we can't allow you to get hurt. So you can't have your crutches in case he uses them to attack you.'

'Don't be so bloody stupid,' I said. 'I know this bloke, he's an old mate of mine. I suppose I'll just have to write to the Governor.'

One thing the screws don't like you doing is writing to the Governor because, under the rules, the Governor has to reply. And what he can't stand is cons flooding him with letters about petty matters. Threatening to write to the boss about something trivial is a final resort, but this time I got my way.

The screw disappeared and a few minutes later was back. 'OK,' he said. 'Stand away from the door. Here are your crutches, but be it on your own head. If he turns, you're in trouble. You've been warned.'

Tony wasn't as crazy as the screws liked to believe but he'd have his moments, like when he would look under the bed or in a drawer and go, 'Come out of there, zebra. Zebra, do what you're told. Zebra, what are you doing?'

I'd say, 'Tony, snap out of it. You're talking to the drawer, mate. Now come on.'

Slowly, I started getting through to Tony and, little by little, he was responding.

But the screws insisted on liquid coshing him all the time.

I tried reasoning with them. 'Look, he's my mate,' I'd say. 'He's all right. Why are you giving him all this Largactil?'

'Because he likes it.'

'No he doesn't.'

Sometimes you can play the ticket inside. If you get four years and don't want to do it, you can pretend you're a madman. And, if you keep it up long enough, you might get a year in a secure unit and then, because you start behaving normally again, you'll get out. But it's a tricky game to play because to do the ticket properly you have to be on Largactil, and before you know it you really do go a little bit off key.

Whether this had been Tony's tactic, I don't know. But I do know that, when he was one of Syd's crew in Lewisham, there was fuck all barmy about him then. The screws used to call Tony a 'fraggle' and I was a 'muppet' because of my disability.

I used to keep on at them about not liquid coshing him so much, but they didn't care. Then, slowly, I started getting through to Tony and he realised it was the Largactil that was making him go off his head. And then, one day, he refused the medication.

'What have you been filling his head with?' one of the screws shouted at me.

'Nothing. Nothing like your fucking Largactil.'

'Well, we're moving you out of this cell.'

'I'm not going. Tony is my mate and we are sticking together.'

'Peter, if I have any more of your lip you'll be straight back down the block.'

Now that was a red rag to me. My life was about not doing things I was told by the screws or the Old Bill. Although I was frightened of the system and frightened of Lewes – I kept thinking I was going to be one of those guys who'd been found in prison 'murdered' – I wasn't frightened of the screws.

'Bring it on, bring the block on,' I hissed at him. 'Let it come.'

Tony had been getting better slowly. He hadn't harmed me, he hadn't even interrupted my sleep, so I didn't know why the screws should get so uptight about everything.

But then two of them burst into the cell and immediately took hold of Tony even though he wasn't freaking out or anything. This made me mad. I thought, Any more of this and my mate really will need Largactil. So I went loopy, I went fucking loopy. It was the first time I realised I could handle two fully grown men. They went to grab me and I jumped up. Bang! I hit one straight in the face while the other one grabbed me from behind to try and restrain me. It had no effect at all. I just shrugged off his hold and, with the help of my crutches, kept them at bay.

'I told you I needed my crutches in here. I knew they'd come in handy,' I said with a smirk.

They both tried to rush me at the same time and I clouted both of them. They paused, looked at each other for a split-second and then legged it out of the cell, banging the door shut behind them.

My first thoughts were for Tony who was down on the floor shaking and babbling on again about zebras and camels.

'It's all right, I won't let them harm you,' I told him. 'It'll be OK.'

But the next thing I knew, four screws burst into the cell. And they were not messing around. They were carrying wet blankets, strait-jackets and rubber coshes. Even I knew I was outnumbered, but I wasn't going to give in.

I looked around the cell and saw our piss-pot on the floor full to the brim. As quick as a flash, I picked it up and hurled it at the four screws, drenching them.

All hell broke loose. Two of them tried to cosh me but I managed to bite the finger of one of them and heard it snap. He screamed in pain and staggered back, but then another one got me on the back of the neck and, as I was starting to fall unconscious, I realised they were manhandling me into a strait-jacket.

I don't remember any more before waking up in a padded cell.

But the real story was Tony. Within days of him eventually getting out of the nick, he went to the Citibank tower in Lewisham, the tallest building in the area. He managed to get right up to the top – 18 floors I think it is – and he threw himself off.

I was devastated when I heard. I went down to Lewisham and I openly wept for Tony, and cursed the reasons that had driven him to do it.

I'd got out of Lewes a long time before then and prison hadn't done me any good. It had made me a harder bastard, a real hardened man.

Prisons to me were just like children's homes and foster homes. They were all part of a system that had dogged me from the day I was born, from the day I was put into care by my own parents and shunted through life from pillar to post.

* * *

After that stint inside, I tried to pick my life up again back down in Limehouse. While having a drink with a few of my mates, I found out that Sherry, whom I'd always been fond of since she took my virginity in Prince's Lodge and who I'd been seeing on and off, had fucked off with some bloke.

That was all right with me because she said that, if she ever got the chance of being with the father of her child, then she'd take it. I wanted to see her for practical reasons. Where was my dog Chub? I thought she'd got him. And how come my squat in Jamaica House had been broken into and burgled while I was inside? It was the second time I had been burgled!

Sherry had gone south of the river but I managed to track her down. I knocked on the door and this big geezer answered. He took one look at me and turned to Sherry who was in the hallway.

'Christ, Sherry,' he said. 'You didn't tell me you were going out with Duchy.' And off he went to pack his bags and leave.

I thought 'My reputation really does go before me.' But I said, 'Hold on, mate, I ain't come here for Sherry. I've come for a bit of information. You're the baby's father. You stay right here.'

So we all had a drink, things got sorted. I knew where Chub was – with one of Linda's mates. And, God bless her heart, Sherry even gave me my bus fare back to the East End.

I was a bit down so I went into the Blue Posts pub to have a drink with my mate Colin aka Slag, head of the chapter, The Family. Colin and his boys were good to me and, like their name, they treated me like family. I then decided to head over the road to Charlie Brown's pub.

As I was crossing the road, I saw a police car coming and I froze. I didn't move until they were only about an arm's length away. They missed me, I don't think they even saw me. But it had shaken me. It was almost as if I had been about to faint at the sight of a police car. It wasn't the Old Bill themselves that bothered me. Bring 'em on. Bring 'em all on. It was what they had come to represent to me.

Prison, I realised, was their weapon. If they wanted to, they could keep me in the nick for as long as they liked. I'd been brought up all my life by people saying, 'Do this, don't do that ...' I had begun to fear the system, the racist system, and the system was dragging me down.

I thought of the Mongols. Whatever the Mongols didn't understand, they despised; whatever they despised, they feared; and whatever they feared, they destroyed.

That was going to be my salvation. I realised I was either going to become institutionalised, or I had to step up my game.

I went for the latter.

7

Rules and Regulations

M Y INTRODUCTION TO bigger-time crime started, strangely enough, with a fairly innocent bag snatch.

I was down in Charlie Brown's, which was starting to look well-faded by then. There was me and one of my friend's daughters. We had a quiet drink and chatted. And then, right at the end of the evening, this black geezer came up, pretended to trip, just about held on to his glass, and he was gone.

'Oi … Oi,' screams the girl. 'He's nicked my purse … he's nicked my bloody purse!'

Pandemonium. We both jumped up off the well-worn banquette, crashed into the table and spilled the drinks, but not before I saw what was going on. It was the old pass-the-parcel scam, and something they must have done many times before. One guy passed the purse to another, who passed it on to his mate, and the final guy sprinted outside and jumped into a parked car.

I smiled, because it was well executed, but I was as angry as hell.

Clat … clat … clat … clat … I got to the car just as this black bloke was trying to start the engine. I could see the purse on the back seat and so I banged on the driver's window as hard as I could.

'That's my fucking friend's purse,' I shouted as the guy was fumbling with the keys in the ignition. 'You've picked on the wrong bloke here, mate.'

With that, I smashed one of the crutches into the window, shattering the glass. I pushed my fist through, grabbed the driver by the throat and hauled him out of the car almost breaking off the door in the process.

He was a big fella who kept shouting, 'Rhaatid. Rass clot, rass clot. A fe me car.'

'I don't care if it is your car, that's my bloody friend's purse you've nicked,' and with that I hit him one so hard it broke his nose; blood was pouring everywhere.

'Blood clot,' he started screaming. 'Blood clot.' So I hit him again. He ran straight back to the pub and grabbed four bottles. There was blood all over him and he was smashing off the ends off the bottles to use them as weapons and come at me. The guy was screaming at the top of his voice in Jamaican patois. I stood my ground, waiting for him to come, when two of his mates jumped on him and held him back. As he was struggling, he was shouting at me, 'Tomorrow me ae deal with you den me mash you up.'

'Yeah, whatever,' I said and calmly leaned into the car, picked up the purse, and went back inside to give it to my friend.

The next night, I was back outside Charlie Brown's again. I knew the geezer would appear because he had a score to settle. I was a bit surprised when I saw him. His nose was all plastered up – and he was carrying a baseball bat, which he must have decided was the best way he could 'mash me up'.

When he saw me, he pointed to my crutches and to his baseball bat and said, 'You have fe your stick, now me have fe mine.'

I realised I would have to knock him out as quickly as possible. Just a glancing blow with the baseball bat and I was a gonna. The odds weren't very good. So I feigned friendliness.

'Come on, mate,' I said. 'I don't want to fight with you. Save it for another day. Let's go and have a drink in the pub over the road.'

He spat on the floor in front of me.

Fair enough, I thought. I guess that meant no. 'Well, I'm going on my own then,' I said and calmly walked past him. He was totally confused and, instead of guarding himself with the baseball bat in front of his chest, he let it drop a little. That was just enough for me to swing round, and one mighty swipe on his wrist forced him to drop the bat.

'My stick now, I think,' I said as I picked up the bat. 'Come on, let's go and have that drink.'

So, grudgingly, he came with me to Charlie Brown's which is just opposite The Blue Posts. Once in there, I was surrounded by plenty of my mates and the geezer was no longer a threat. By the end of the evening, my mates had even convinced him that I was OK. But, as a word of advice, they told him that I should never be messed with.

While all that was going on, a black guy with long dreadlocks came up to me. I'd seen him in the Posts and Charlie Brown's a few times, but I had never spoken to him. He had such a strong Jamaican accent that I couldn't understand a word he was saying and kept asking him to speak slower.

What I think he was saying was, 'I watched you fight yesterday and it was quite impressive. Aren't you scared?'

'No,' I said, hoping it was the right answer.

I had never really hung around with Jamaican people before. All my upbringing, apart from when I was with the guys from The 37ᵗʰ Temple at Prince's Lodge, had been with white people. I spoke with a white accent to such a degree that even the blacks I knew used to call me Bounty – black on the outside, white on the inside.

But the more I spoke with the dreadlocked guy in the pub, the more I realised me and him weren't that different, even if most of the time I didn't know what he was going on about.

That evening, I went with him to his flat. I'd got my place back at Jamaica House but I was still trying to get it ship-shape after it had been burgled while I was in the nick. He kept saying to me, 'Yo must walk, man, yo must walk with something.' I still couldn't understand what he was going on about, but he kept saying, 'Yo need something, yo must walk.'

And then I realised what he meant – a gun.

'Now hold on,' I said. 'I don't need a gun. I can punch most people out; I've got my *nunchukas* and my martial arts' skills; I can walk up walls, spin on me crutches. I don't need no gun, mate, I don't need no gun.'

'The man'll hurt yo. Yo must walk, yo must walk with a gun,' he kept repeating.

The next evening, I saw the dreadlocked guy again down by Charlie Brown's and he had a very quiet but angry look on his face.

'Why didn't ya meet me, man, why didn't ya meet me?' he said.

'What do you mean, "meet you"?' I asked.

'Me tell y0 fe meet me h at six o'clock … me tell you fe meet na de Londoner.'

I couldn't remember agreeing to anything like that, but then again, because his Jamaican patois was so strong, I couldn't understand half of what he was going on about.

Evidently, he had been waiting for me outside the Londoner pub and he had brought me a gun even though I had specifically told him that I didn't want one. While he was waiting for me, the Old Bill stopped him on suspicion and searched his bag but they did not find the gun. The poor cunt shit himself. He was fuming as if it was my fault. I calmed him down and explained again that I didn't want a gun and I had no need to carry one.

'OK, you don't like gun,' he said. 'But your friend, he like gun.'

And that's when I thought he might be right. Maybe I did know a few people who might need one.

That's when I knew I was on the road to meeting people who could supply me with guns that I could sell, and I realised this move would take me out of the shadows of petty crime. I'd started to raise my game. But, wherever I got my guns from, I was always told, almost like it was some sort of mantra, 'Don't sell guns to black boys … don't sell guns to black boys.' Blacks were irresponsible when it came to handling guns. They were far too trigger-happy.

I was hanging around with lots of black guys back then because there was a culture of black music in the clubs that I loved. And black guys with their music boxes and speakers would challenge each other in a thing called a sound clash. The sounds that would turn up were trojan Jashucker and Sledgehammer.

For some reason, probably because of my English accent, they used to look down on me. As well as 'Bounty', they'd call me 'Coconut' and all sorts of names. But they'd always want me to help them out in way or another.

'Look, I've got trouble tonight,' one of them would say. 'Duch, can you sharpen my knife for me?'

And I'd sharpen his knife or I'd sharpen his sword. But I never told them about the guns I had.

London, even in those days in the Eighties, was awash with guns. You could get your hands on just about anything, although nowhere near as cheap as they are today. There were sawn-off shotguns, small snub-nose pistols, little .22s. But mostly it was sawn-off shotguns, usually the hammer-head. The reason the hammer-head was so liked was because you could load it safely. With the later models, like the under over, once you loaded it and closed the barrel, all you had to do was pull the trigger and the gun would fire. If you did not have the safety, on unlike the hammerhead, you had to pull the hammer back before it went 'bang bang'.

Side-by-side barrelled shotguns were the cheapest because they were older than the over-and-under ones. But automatics were also very popular because they were a single barrel where you put the cartridge in the tube and shot off lots of rounds quickly instead of having to stop and reload all the time. Back then, you'd pay between £200 and £300 for a decent sawn-off, but now you can pick one up for £50 if you know the right people.

Pub owners, club owners and businessmen around Mile End in the East End all wanted their own guns for protection. But, most of the time, I'd be renting out guns to villains. It was £75 to hire one for a day, but if the gun got fired then you had to buy it. It was more lucrative for me to rent out guns than to sell them.

Post office blags were fairly common, although, with increased security, inexperienced kids were finding it harder to rob even the most basic sub-post office.

'Duch,' they'd complain to me. 'I don't know what it is but as soon as we even approach a post office it seems the shutters go up and the alarm goes off. Even when we pull out a shooter it doesn't scare 'em. Maybe we need a better gun.'

'What you've got's fine,' I'd say. 'It's how you're approaching the blag that's all wrong.'

'What do you mean?'

'Well, pulling on a balaclava, walking into the post office and brandishing a sawn-off might look good on the television. But that's where it should stay. These post-masters are trained to secure anything within seconds of there being even the slightest hint of trouble. What you've got to do is outsmart them.'

'How do we do that?'

'Come back here tomorrow evening and I'll show you.'

My whole status in the area was changing rapidly because of the power of the guns I could get hold of. The Pakistani corner shopkeepers were constantly in trouble with kids coming in and stealing from them. They knew who the thieves were but couldn't do anything about it. So I'd collar the kids and give them a talking to and, as if by magic, the shoplifting would stop.

Everyone knew it was best not to mess with Duchy and so my reputation as a 'Regulator' around that part of the East End began to grow.

The Pakistani shopkeepers were so pleased they would even give me free bags of food to show how grateful they were.

People were coming to me for advice. They were asking me if I could 'have a quiet word' with someone about a deal that might have gone a bit wrong. And so I sorted things out and, although I was still a fighter, it was rare that I had to resort to my fists.

Just the fact that Duch had had a word with you was enough for most people to see the error of their ways.

As a Regulator, I liked to keep my little patch fairly trouble-free. The last thing I wanted was for the villains to start fighting amongst themselves. And after a while, they came to respect that.

Clat … clat … clat … clat … wasn't just a sound that came to be feared in that part of London, it was also the sound of street justice.

The following day, the boys came back to find out the secret of a successful post office blag.

'So go on then, Duchy, how do we outsmart them?'

'Well, for a start,' I said, 'you can ditch those balaclavas. You might as well paint a sign saying "Nick me" on your forehead as wear one of them. Instead, you dress up in these.' I threw them a couple of uniforms.

'What are they?'

'Have a look.'

'Christ, Duchy, they're postman's uniforms.'

'Exactly. You wear those and you enter the post office with the gun hidden. I guarantee you, not only will the sub-postmaster smile as if he recognises you, he will also open the hatch for you to collect the parcels from behind the counter.

'At that point, you stick the gun through. He'll be too petrified to make any move, let alone go for an alarm button.'

'Wow, Duch, that's a great idea,' said one of the enthusiastic kids.

'Oh, and by the way,' I replied. 'That's £50 each for the hire of the uniforms. And don't get them dirty or you'll have the dry cleaning bill to pay as well.'

I didn't know how much they would get from a blag, it varied, but there was so much of it going on that I was renting out guns all the time.

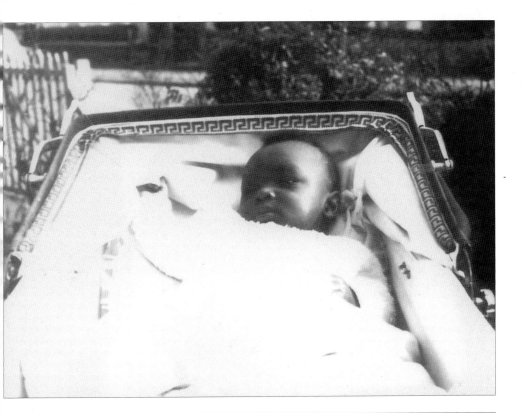

Me as a baby, sweet and innocent.

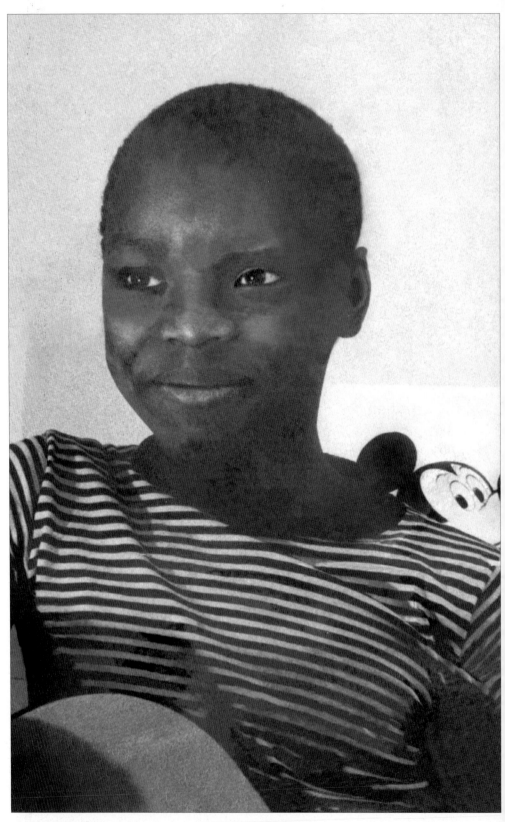

Me as a kid, when I was living with the Rodriguez family.

My beautiful dogs. *Main picture*:
Samson and Kizzie.

Inset: Chub, the bad boy.

Giving martial arts demonstrations in south London.

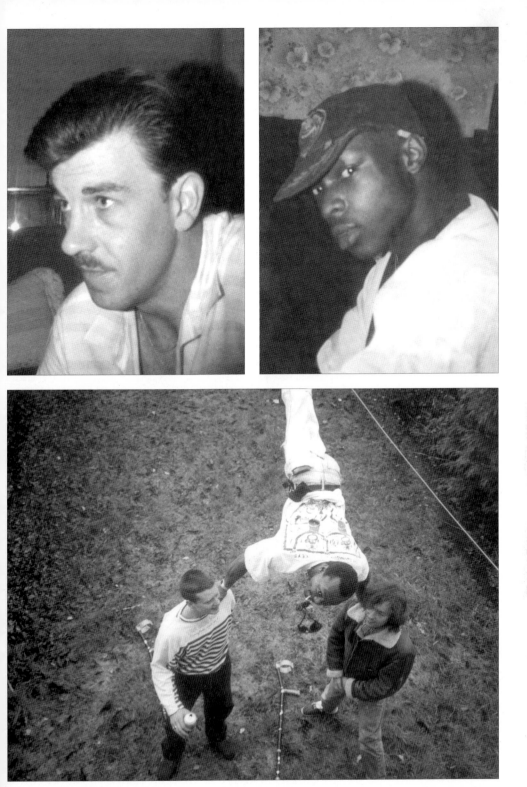

Above left: Charlie Hooper, one of my closest friends.

Above right: Chilling out at home in Brockley.

Below: Demonstrating my upper body strength.

My beautiful kids. *Above left*: Dean, my son.

Above right: My daughter Jade.

Below: Dean and Jade when they were toddlers.

In the studio, making my music with my band Harlequin.

With my friend Stilks, one of the best doormen in London and, *below*, Stilks with me and Jane.

I was still getting them through my Jamaican connections, but I know for a fact they were actually coming from a white guy up in Camden Town, North London. But I didn't ask too many questions.

The centre for all the skulduggery was a well-known pub and there was a big biker crowd that used to gather there. There was nothing bikers liked better than getting drunk and taking a few Blues. I had an excellent connection for amphetamines and so I could supply them with plenty of Blues. They were a big, hard, tough bunch. And there was always one who might have had too much snakebite and would want to take a pop at me.

I remember one night this biker saying, 'Look, I know you think you're hard but I'll take you and your dog outside and I'll smash you up.'

Obviously, he didn't know much about Chub.

So I replied, 'Forget it, mate, you couldn't even beat the dog.'

We ended up outside. He was a monster of a bloke with long hair and tattoos. There was a beer in one hand, a joint in the other, and he was talking out of his arse.

'I don't even need to put me beer down to take you on,' he jeered.

Here we go again, I thought.

So I pulled one out so fast I hit him twice on the nose – bop, bop – before he even managed to square up. Breaking noses was becoming a bit of a trademark of mine. But, if you hit the nose squarely first time, it means your opponent has no eyesight. And, once the eyesight has gone, you can go for the kidneys and close him down, which is exactly what I did.

That was my initiation into the bikers' scene and Colin, who was the head of the Chapter, took a real shine to me and I even began to see myself riding with them … well, almost. The bikers used to give me bags of white powder, which I would pass on to my mate until he ended up getting nicked for having cocaine in his wallet.

The East End was changing at the time, with guns becoming more widespread and more people wanting them. And the only way to stay alive was to stay ahead.

Only a few years before, if you needed a gun or a knife to go and deal with someone, you were regarded as a coward. Most problems were sorted out by people fighting with their fists. But times were rapidly changing. It wasn't simply a question of hiring a gun for £75 a day any more; those guns were being used more and more in gangland killings.

I got scared after someone was murdered and two brothers came to see me. They wanted a showdown with this other firm of black guys and they wanted me to provide the weapons and ammunition.

But I remembered the first lesson I had learned – don't sell guns to black boys. And I stuck to it.

'Sorry, no can do,' I told them.

'What do you mean, Duch, "no can do"?'

'I'm not renting or selling you any guns and that's the end of it.'

'Well, we'll see about that,' one of them shouted at me. 'Keep looking over your shoulder, Duch.'

'Don't anger me and don't threaten me,' I replied as calmly as possible. 'Now go.'

They realised I was a lot more powerful than them because I had control of the guns, but things were starting to escalate.

I didn't care whether any of the guns I provided were used in major crimes and I didn't want to know. That was none of my business. But what I didn't want to do was spark an unnecessary killing spree amongst two-bit firms who thought they were hard bastards because they were hiding behind sawn-off shotguns. I was hearing about martial artists, great fighters, who were just getting murdered, shot stone dead, by some 20-year-old who couldn't fight to save his life.

That's when I started carrying a .22 pistol. It's a simple, inexpensive blowback gun with fixed sights which has low recoil and uses cheap ammunition. It was really just for close quarters and, although I never had recourse to use it, I would have done if the circumstances had arisen. Make no mistake about that.

I was still living in Jamaica House at the time and, because my persona had changed and I was getting respect as a Regulator, I gave up singing in the clubs and pubs. My mum and dad didn't come to see me again and I never got in touch with them, although the big question I wanted answering was always at the back of my mind. The only people who ever took an interest in me were the police. They were nicking me on a regular basis for fighting, carrying a knife, all the usual stuff. Thank God they didn't know about the guns. I was in and out of prison all the time. I went back to Lewes, down to Rochester, all over the place.

The strange thing was that when I was out of circulation for a few months at a time, the street crime around Limehouse used to go up because there was no one to regulate what went on. Most of the stuff I dealt with was petty anyway, but it kept people in check.

The majority of times I'd just say to someone, 'Now, you know that belongs to him. Why did you fucking take it? Now give it back.'

And for some reason it worked. People feared me. They

feared me and they feared Chub who had turned into quite a psychotic dog. With a dog like that, they never knew what frame of mind they might find me in.

Between stretches in prison, I managed to keep my flat going in Jamaica House and that's where an old mate of mine named Kevin turned up one night.

'Duch,' he said, 'I need a gun.'

Now Kevin wasn't the brightest of blokes, but I reckoned he would be all right and I agreed to rent him a sawn-off shotgun.

'Doncha want to know why I need it, Duch?'

'None of my business, mate.'

He seemed a bit agitated, a bit nervous.

'I'll tell you anyway. I'm going to shoot a bloke.'

I wished he hadn't told me, but now it was out there was nothing I could do about it.

'In which case,' I said, 'I don't want the gun back. You'll have to buy it and get rid of it as soon as you can after firing it.'

'Where's the best place to do that then, Duch?'

I was slowly being drawn in. I let out a big sigh.

'OK, Kevin,' I said, 'sit down. Now where are you going to do this shooting?'

It was planned for Whitechapel. So I worked out a route for Kevin. I told him he had to go down Salmon Lane, into Commercial Road, then run down the canal footpath and throw the gun into Limehouse Basin. Then we could meet back at my place in Jamaica House.

So it was decided that Kevin should go on a practice run so we could see just how much time was needed for him to pull the trigger and get back to my flat.

'I don't want to kill him,' explained Kevin nervously. 'I just want to hurt him.'

'As I said, that's none of my business. Now let's try this dummy run.'

So Kevin went over to Whitechapel, checked the time and started back down to Limehouse. He was back very quickly, which was fast enough for him to get away from the scene of the crime and dump the gun.

'OK, Kevin,' I said. 'That time seems fine. Where's the gun?'

'The gun, Duch?

'Yeah, the gun.'

'I threw it in Limehouse Basin like you told me to.'

I held my head in my hands.

'You fucking dummy,' I yelled. 'You're not supposed to do that until you've shot the geezer, you useless pillock.'

'Sorry, Duch, I thought we could get the gun out of the Basin later.'

As I mentioned, he wasn't top of his class at school.

But now I had a real problem because I had to get my hands on another gun for the job to be finished. But the only one I could get was a totally inadequate side-by-side shotgun. This wasn't a fucking robbery, it was a shooting! The gun was shit. I would never have even fired it.

Kevin ended up paying twice and I still don't know whether he shot the bloke or not because he never came back to my flat like we had arranged.

Shootings rather than hold-ups were now becoming regular occurences and if a shooting was arranged you can guarantee it was something to do with me. I knew about all the shootings even though I kept telling everyone it was none of my business. Some people who are going to shoot someone else seem to have this compulsion to tell, to share what they are going to do.

I knew most of the victims deserved every bit of lead they

got because they were getting too big for their boots. But you can't run around in London and just shoot anybody. You have to know what you are doing or you have problems. The shootings were always in the gangland fraternity, never outside it. And, whether the people were shot dead or merely injured, I didn't really care.

Some people who came for guns were actually scared of them and that made them an even bigger liability. If you are frightened of them it makes you dangerous to be around and you'll end up shooting someone by mistake. I've known villains shoot their own toes off, or shoot their mate. But that was mainly those who didn't want to pay for a good hammer-head shotgun.

I was never frightened of the people I was renting or selling guns to, never frightened of them at all. But I have to admit that I have hurt people myself. If I got murdered tomorrow on my own doorstep, I wouldn't know what it was for. There are probably people looking for me now, but it doesn't worry me. You can't afford to let it worry you. What I did, I did then. Now I am a totally changed person but that doesn't excuse all the things I did. I was not a nice person to know when I was in my twenties and I recognise that now. But it would still be a few years before I realised that it was possible to escape the mad downward spiral of crime. It would take love and an enormous tragedy to pull me to my senses, force me to take stock of my life and understand that I couldn't go on forever blaming my real parents, my foster parents, children's homes, Social Services and prison for the way my life had turned out. But, for the moment, there seemed no way out. I didn't even seem to have a fighting chance.

I started working in an illegal club set up in a nearby block of flats. It was really two flats but the adjoining wall had been knocked down to make it into a club. I'd never go there for a decent night's entertainment now. It was a terrible place. Every night someone got cut up. But the guy who ran the place was looking for someone to work on the door. It was a blues club which would also play lots of reggae and was open until ridiculous hours of the morning.

It was only £1 to get in the club but no one even wanted to pay that.

'Pay to come in here?' said one Jamaican guy incredulously. '*Yo* pay *me* to come in here.'

I sighed. 'Have you paid, mate?' I asked quietly.

'Raas clot.'

So I said to him calmly, 'I asked you a simple question and you are giving it monkey bollocks.' With that I stepped outside and pulled out my *nunchukas*. When the Jamaican realised I was serious, he pleaded with me not to fight. So I put the *nunchukas* on the floor and said, 'Listen, mate, I don't care if you've paid or not. But don't embarrass me like that again.'

If there was one thing I couldn't stand in those days it was being disrespected. I felt as if I had been disrespected all my life, but I had pulled myself up to become the local Regulator in and around Limehouse. And that deserved respect, and I demanded it.

I don't know why I took the door job at the club because I hated the place. The nightly stabbings would be over ridiculous things like someone stepping on someone's shoes or spilling a drink in the packed, dark, smoky club. And the black guys were continually asking me to sell them guns. No way.

I remember spilling some juice on one geezer's shoes and he came over to me to clean it off. Obviously, I refused, so he said he was going to clean it off by kicking me up the arse.

I told him that, if I hit him first, he wouldn't be in a fit state to clean his shoes let alone kick someone.

I remember looking at him and thinking, You're an old man. You should be home with your grandchildren, not in a squalid club giving it large to someone like me who you don't even know.

That was the problem. Because I was disabled, people who didn't know me had no respect for me. He's just a cripple, he's useless, is what most of them thought.

I still get it now until someone steps up to them and whispers in their ear that the game they are playing is not a very clever one, and that I am Duchy and they will lose.

Strangely enough, one of the few people who treated me civilly was the local community copper. All my grown-up life I had been fighting the police. I never really had a chance to fight stupid idiots in the street to the same degree that I was constantly fighting the Old Bill. As I've said, they called me Hercules down the local nick and genuinely despised me. I'd constantly be taken in for possessing an offensive weapon – my knife. And I'd tell them, 'It doesn't matter how many times you stop me, because I always carry a knife.' They despaired of me, but thankfully they never raided my flat. They never found the guns.

Ray, the community copper, treated me differently. He was friendly and he'd say, 'They're whingeing about you again down the station, Duch. Why don't you knock it on the head, mate. Then we can all have an easy time.'

He had quiet authority and, although he knew all the things I'd done and the constant petty prison sentences I endured, he still treated me as a human being. Ray was the first person in my life, since I'd been a baby with Ian and June Coward, who impressed me.

But he couldn't make me go straight and I soon got banged

up again. I was on a merry-go-round between Lewes, Rochester and Latchmere House in Surrey. As soon as the merry-go-round stopped, I'd be back in Limehouse and you can bet my flat had been broken into again in my absence.

It was all turning into a nightmare. As a Regulator, people thought I could solve everything. This geezer told me that his brother-in-law had been noncing his daughter and could I do something about it? Obviously, a talking-to wasn't going to be sufficient. So at six o'clock one morning, I went round to the brother-in-law's house with the geezer, a rubber hose and a piece of barbed wire. We used the rubber hose to beat the granny out of the bloke and stuck the barbed wire up his arse. I'm not pleased with what I did; it was all part of the East End madness.

After my flat in Jamiaca House had been burgled again while I was in prison, I decided that was it. I went down to Charlie Brown's and told my mates.

'You're doing what, Duch?' said one of them. 'You can't, you're part of Limehouse. You belong here.'

'No I don't and yes I can,' I replied. 'I'm going back south of the river. I'm going home.'

8

The Face Fits Down South

DON'T GET ME wrong, I had no intention of 'going home' to see my parents in Forest Hill. That was all still unresolved. The people I visited first were Social Services to see if they could find me somewhere to live in South London. It took about four weeks for a letter to come through from them and, in the meantime, I'd been kipping on the floor at a flat belonging to one of my old biker mates.

'Have they got you anywhere, Duch?' asked my mate hopefully as I tore open the envelope. He was a good geezer but four weeks is pushing it with anyone.

'Yeah they have,' I replied. 'But it's the poxy Honor Oak Estate in Brockley Rise.'

'Oh, that's brilliant.'

No it fucking well wasn't. I remembered the estate from when I was a kid and used to pass through it. They were pre-war flats and it was derelict then. I remember the windows being all smashed in and thinking at the time that it was like a war zone. The last thing I ever expected was to be living there, but now it looked like I was – at 68 Barville Close. Well, at least it had windows, but it was still a one-bedroom shit-hole.

I didn't have anything to take with me. No cooker, nothing. The burglars at Jamaica House had done a good job that last time. It was the first time I felt proper loneliness, but fortunately my new next-door neighbours, John and Sue, took pity on me for the first few weeks. They hadn't got much themselves but they were good, kind, salt-of-the-earth people who would share whatever they had.

Then, one day, there was a knock on the door and there were my old mates Trent Thomas, Rob and Freddy, the guys from The 37th Temple. It gave me the lift I needed to stop wondering if I'd made the wrong decision. All my old mates came round at one time or another, including a guy named Jez whom I'd met towards the end of my stay in Jamaica House.

I'd got to know him through a biker girl I'd been dating at the time called Kim. He was a good-looking bloke who was never short of women and ended up getting involved with a lovely girl from Limehouse named Carron who had a lot going for her, and he eventually married her.

Jez was into racketeering and prostitution and was running a string of girls in Earl's Court.

'Jez,' I said, quite startled when I opened the door at Barville Close. 'What the fuck are you doing here? It's great to see you.'

'Well, you couldn't hide from me, Duchy.'

And so we got talking.

'I was wondering if you might be into doing a bit of stickering for me,' he said, 'and I'll need a bit of muscle to keep the girls protected.'

I was short of cash at the time and so I agreed to do the West End telephone boxes while I got myself back on my feet.

I got to meet many of the girls and I really got on with them. Some of them were real stunners. But to Jez they were just a commodity and I didn't like the way he was treating them. Some pimps can be real good to their girls and others can be right bastards. I had a feeling about which way Jez played it. But it was nothing to do with me and socially we got on really well.

One day, he introduced me to this girl named Michelle, who was a friend of his cousin.

She was an absolute stunner with dark sultry looks, bags of style, and she was well educated. I didn't stand a chance.

Although I'd had my fair share of girlfriends since Sherry taught me the ropes, I was always a little apprehensive when introduced to anyone new. I didn't know whether they might pity me for my disability rather than like me for myself. But I had no qualms with Michelle; we hit it off together straight away.

We did the usual things, going for a drink and that, and naturally she asked me about my mum and dad.

I told her they lived in Forest Hill and explained all about my upbringing and how I didn't really get on with my dad because they had abandoned me at birth and never really told me why.

'I'm sure they had their reasons, Duch,' she said quietly.

'Maybe, but he's a bloody vicar, for God's sake! It would have to be a pretty good reason to dump one of his kids because he was born handicapped.'

'Perhaps you don't know the full story,' replied Michelle.

She was like that. She would always try to see both sides of an argument. And so we started going out. It was the most wonderful time of my life and I had great visions of our future together. I began to think Michelle might be the one person who could turn my life around. I wanted to have kids with her, I wanted to settle down in Brockley Rise and I wanted to get back on the straight and narrow. And, believe it or not, most, but not all of it, would come true.

So, when Michelle innocently asked why I hadn't introduced her to my mum and dad, I thought, Yeah, why haven't I? Why not?

I didn't want the Return of the Prodigal Son to be too much of a shock for my parents. After all, I hadn't seen them since they came to visit me in Jamaica House, so I phoned Mum first and asked if it would be all right to come round the following Sunday.

'Mum … Mum, are you still there?' I shouted down the phone because everything had gone quiet.

'Of course I am, son. I was just a bit shocked to hear your voice. We'd love to see you on Sunday. I'll tell your dad. Oh, what a great surprise.' And I could hear that she was genuinely happy.

I was quite apprehensive about the visit but it seemed to go off all right and they warmed to Michelle as soon as they met her. Mind you, she had told me to be on my best behaviour and not to rake up the past. This, she said, was a new beginning and I had to look at it like that.

Dad was also more pleasant than usual, with none of his laying down the rules. I think Mum must have had a word with him as well. And, of course, the big question was never broached.

I must say I was relieved when it was all over.

'I need a drink, Michelle,' I said as we walked away. 'They serve too much tea in that house.' And we both laughed.

Michelle's mum lived in a small town house in Brixton, filled with the finest antiques. Her dad had provided well for the family but I never did meet him or speak to him until much later in our relationship, because I heard he was not very happy with his daughter going out with someone like me. But her mum treated me with kindness and respect.

Michelle had told me earlier that her dad, George Cauana, worked in the entertainment industry. And I just left it at that. Now I realised exactly who he was. He ran casinos, snooker halls and pool halls throughout London and had amassed a fortune.

I also learned later, after talking to friends, that he had been on a hit-list drawn up by the Krays. They had tried to blow him up in a Mini outside George's house. It is all detailed in the book *Profession of Violence* by John Pearson.

After the whirlwind of meeting Mrs Cauana, it was only when I sat down that it dawned on me – I was getting involved with a big-timer's daughter.

And I had to pinch myself. Michelle wasn't the usual white girl who went out with black guys. She was well spoken and had a good job; she was a beautiful girl, a perfect woman and a virgin.

So I was gobsmacked when Michelle suggested she move in with me at Barville Close.

'You're joking, ain't you?' I said. 'Why do you want to move from the warmth and safety of you mum's to live with someone like me?

'Because I'll be with you, silly.'

I had to pinch myself again.

I'd promised myself to go on the straight and narrow after I met Michelle … but I couldn't. For a start, there would be no money to treat her, plus I'd been putting a little firm together myself since I'd moved south of the river and I didn't want to disappoint all those guys.

I was still working with Jez and his prostitutes and one

day he asked me to call him because he was having a bit of trouble. I needed to see him anyway. I wanted to buy a car and needed to get back to Limehouse and see Barry Adams, part of North London's Adams family, who ran a garage under the arches there.

So we jumped into Jez's Chrysler and went up there, where Barry had a great Jag for sale. As I was looking around the car with Barry's dad, he took me to one side and whispered, 'Be careful with that Jez. Watch him. That's all I'm saying.'

I had always felt a bit uneasy about how flash Jez was, but we were friends. Why on earth would Barry Adams's want to warn me about him?

I didn't think too much about it as I drove over to Earl's Court with Jez that night. But when we got to his house there was something different going on, something wasn't quite right. His wife, Carron, was as beautiful as ever but she looked more flamboyant than usual. The make-up, the hair, the clothes were all just that bit over-the-top.

'Is Carron going out somewhere?' I asked casually.

'Oh, she's part of the firm now,' explained Jez. 'She goes round to pick up all the money off the girls and this and that.'

So Carron picked up her handbag and coat, and we decided to wait for her to come back before going out to a few clubs.

'I wanted a word with you, Duchy,' said Jez. 'I've been having trouble with a few punters recently. Nothing serious, but it alarms the girls. Wondered if you could keep an extra eye out for me. A bit of muscle.'

'Sure.'

And so we waited for Carron. One hour … two hours … three hours. At seven o'clock in the morning, Jez was irate. 'Where is the fucking bitch? … Where is the fucking bitch?' he kept mumbling.

And then the phone went. It was Carron – hysterical, crying, shouting, everything.

'Where are you?' asked Jez.

'Earl's Court tube station,' she managed to blurt out.

We shot straight over. Carron was in a complete state and practically incoherent. She was shaking and her clothes were dishevelled. She took a sly glance at me and then blurted out everything to Jez. She said she had been kidnapped and raped by some Indian guys while she was on her rounds. As she was telling her story, she kept furtively glancing at me and then back to Jez.

I knew there was something wrong with the story. Where had they taken her? Where had the rape taken place? She didn't say.

We managed to get back to Jez's house where Carron took a long bath while we discussed whether or not to call the police. That was a non-starter to begin with, considering all the things we were messed up in.

Later that morning, Jez went out, ostensibly to check on his girls, and Carron, who by this time had calmed herself down, came and sat by me.

'It's hell, Duchy. I'm leaving him,' were her first words.

'But why?'

'Oh, you don't know the half of it.'

'No, but I think I can guess.'

'Can you?'

'You weren't collecting off the girls tonight, were you?'

And that's when she told me everything, the full shocking truth. Jez had put his own wife on the game.

'He threatened me if I didn't do it,' Carron explained as tears flowed. 'But I've had enough. I loved him so much once ... now it's over.'

I decided I had to pull away from Jez. Anyone who

prostitutes his own wife is about as low as you can get. OK, Jez had introduced me to Michelle and for that I was pretty grateful. But I didn't owe him, I didn't owe him at all.

But as much as I tried to distance myself from Jez – I gave up doing muscle for the girls and stickering – the more he seemed to be coming round to Barville Close.

Then, one day, he came around and said, 'You won't believe this, Duchy, but she's left me. Carron's gone and left me. I don't now what I'm gonna do.'

I just looked at him and said, 'You know damn well you had this coming.' And that's when he realised I knew everything.

It was the parting of our ways.

I had also begun to see less of Trent Thomas, Freddy and the rest of The 37th Temple, but my own little firm was starting to grow. I was into the thing I knew best – selling puff.

One day, I came home at about 3.00 pm to see these two guys shaping up to each other in the street. Naturally, I went to get involved. Clat … clat … clat … clat …

'What's going on here?' I said.

'Nothing I can't handle,' replied this vulnerable-looking guy. 'You stay out of it.'

'He dun rob me, he dun rob me,' shouted the Rastafarian who was arguing with him.

'I ain't staying out of nothing,' I replied. 'This is my patch and you two are causing a disturbance.'

'Fuck off,' they both shouted at once.

It transpired that the kid had given the Rastafarian his car to be fixed, but while he was making the repair it seems the Jamaican guy had nicked the car's good starter motor and replaced it with an old one. The kid knew this because he knew what his starter motor looked like and they got into a row over it. In the street. In the night.

'Give me back my starter motor,' he screamed.

'You want your starter motor?' said the Rastafarian, who went to the boot of his car and pulled out this huge jack which he began to swing around his head. 'Start with this,' he yelled.

The young guy ducked and went to the back of his car and pulled out a fucking roof rack. I thought, Christ this one is shaping up.

He lunged at the Rastafarian, warning him first, 'If I hit you on your temple with this roof rack it's going to kill you stone dead.'

That's when I intervened. I said to them, 'This looks mad in the street … why don't you come round the corner and sort it out?'

So they did and the black guy says to the kid, 'I'm not frightened of you, little man, I'm not frightened of you,' and puts his hands in his pockets. I thought he might be going for a knife and so did the kid, who, as quick as lightning, put his hand in the Rastafarian's same pocket and pulled out the guy's hand. He had a knife on the end of a key-ring and the kid, using tremendous force, managed to turn the Rastafarian's hand and stick the knife under his chin.

'Where's my starter motor?' he said

And that's how I met my mate Eugene, a great guy. We became friends and I soon realised I could trust him. He became part of the firm. We drank, we talked and we trained together. We were up at Hilly Fields, a huge park situated between Ladywell and Brockley, at 7.00am every day. He was a good fighter but I felt there was more he had not told me. Later, he mentioned he had been in the Army for nine years before getting kicked out for dishonourable conduct. That explained why he was a nutter.

I met another of the team while I was out walking the dogs. Linda had once again been looking after Chub while I was doing bird but this time she would only let me have him back if I paid her £80. I did that and I got myself a Doberman, and used to walk them round the estate.

One night, while I was out strolling, I saw this small guy who was also walking his dog, a big black one, who I later found out was called Bobby. The guy had a leather jacket on, was a bit cocky, a bit mouthy and came up to me and said, 'You sell a bit of puff, doncha?'

'What's it got to do with you?'

'I do a bit meself. My name's Craig Walters. Me and me dad, this is our manor'

I thought, That's what you think. But I didn't say anything.

Craig introduced me to his dad, who was a very big bloke. And they became a solid part of the firm. I couldn't have controlled Brockley the way I did without them.

Then there was Winston. One day, I went down the road with my dogs to get some chips. I tied the dogs up outside the chip shop and, while I was in there, I heard them barking and growling. I stepped outside to find this black guy saying to his mate, 'Them dogs look pretty vicious. I wonder who they belong to?'

'They're my fucking dogs,' I said. 'What's it got to do with you?'

He took one look at me – dressed in black and pointing with a crutch – and he didn't say a word. That's how I started my friendship with Winston.

We were a tightly knit team who worked well together. We would collect dope from Brixton and divide it into saleable amounts and each member of the team had their own area in which to deal. I was continuing my relationship with Michelle and everything seemed OK.

Then, one day, we were cutting up the gear when the doorbell went. I opened it and there was Jez and his wife

Carron. I hadn't seen them for a long time and thought, What the fuck's going on here? I believed they were out of my life.

Carron looked in a bad way, as if she had had some sort of operation.

I just stared at Jez.

'Duchy, we need somewhere to stay,' he blurted out.

'But I don't have any room,' I started to say.

'Please, it won't be for long. We don't have anywhere to go and Carron's got to rest.'

I never asked what had happened to Carron, whether it had been a botched abortion or what. And I never asked why on earth she had gone back to Jez after she had left him. But they both looked pretty pitiful, and so, reluctantly, Michelle and I gave up our bedroom for them.

By this time, another great bloke named Mark Rider had also joined the firm. All the guys were there that night helping sort out the gear, and they all looked at me with suspicion on their faces. They were very uneasy about the sudden appearance of Jez – who was this bloke? Where did he come from?

'I know what you are all thinking,' I explained, 'but he is not part of the firm and he hasn't come here to oust any of you. He's a mate of mine from the days when I was in the East End.'

They all started talking at once. 'Well, he can't stay here, Duchy, he'll know too much ...' How do you know we can trust him?' 'He looks fucking slippery to me with that suit and all ...'

In a way, they were right. Jez was the slipperiest bastard I had ever met. But he was no grass, and he was smooth and he was convincing. One day, he took me to one side and said, 'Duchy, I'm building everything back up. Forget fucking Earl's Court, I've got some girls over in the East End now and I want you to help me, like it was with us.'

'I don't want anything to do with it, Jez. I've got my own little firm and that's fine by me.'

'Come on, Duchy. For old time's sake. Let me show you the girls.'

So, reluctantly, I went with him back to Limehouse. And that's when I realised just how sad Jez had become. I saw one bloke talking to one of the girls as if he was a punter. And then the next minute I saw the geezer walk away and step into a police car. Jez had lost his patch, he had lost everything and he had deep problems. Eventually, when Carron was looking a bit better, I had to tell them it was time for them to move on.

Throughout this time, Michelle was wonderful, and she encouraged me to take up the guitar again – and write my own songs.

It was like we were a proper unit. I'd sit and sing a few tunes and Michelle would just look up at me and smile. It was simple but we were happy.

The only blot on the landscape was the need to make more money. No doubt, the boys would have come to the rescue if I'd wanted, and Michelle's mum was always giving us lovely presents, but I didn't want to be beholden to her parents. If Michelle had decided to be with me, then it was me who had to look after her.

Things weren't helped because there was another guy on the estate named Sammy, who had a little firm, and he was as keen to get puff on the street as I was. It was a battle. He lived on one side of the estate and I lived on the other and we were both trying to set the record straight as to who was selling the most.

I needed to come up in the world, I needed a bit more

oomph. Guns were no longer a big thing for me. The fact I was once able to sell someone a shooter was neither here nor there. Down in Brockley Rise, I would be more inclined to come round and batter you with my crutches than shoot you with a gun.

I dealt with the business threat from Sammy quite easily after we had a row over a car battery and my dogs pinned him to the wall. He could hardly speak with all the shit in his pants. 'Call the dogs off,' he begged. And then I realised he was finished as any form of opposition.

But I still needed to buy gear in big quantities and that meant going to Brixton in South London. Down there, some of the strong men were Frank Driscoll, Billy, Ricky and Bobby. It was all right going down there and it was all right getting the dope, but I had also heard of guys who ended up getting robbed on their way back.

By this time, I'd got two Dobermans and I decided to fit them with massive special collars that could hold large quantities of puff. With everything ready, I jumped in the Jag with the dogs and set off for Railton Road, which is the centre of all the action in Brixton.

Dealers were lined up on both sides of the street. There was a house called the White House where Frank and Ricky lived and there was the Blue House, home of other notorious suppliers.

All eyes were on the Jag as I moved slowly down the road. I pulled to a halt and got out. Clat … clat … clat … clat … The two huge Dobermans jumped out beside me. They were well trained and didn't need leads. They just walked one each side of me like in *Magnum PI*. It was an impressive sight.

I went up to one of the guys on the street and told him I wanted to buy some of his draw. He showed me a £10 deal, which I contemptuously knocked out of his hand.

'Hey, mon,' he said, 'ya can' be doin' that.'

But, before he could go for a knife or anything, I went eyeball-to-eyeball with him and hissed, 'I mean quantity.' And, as if on cue, both of the Dobermans growled.

The street dealer backed off as I added lightly, 'And I need a free sample.'

The way to make your mark in an unfamiliar situation is to be totally confident and get people to respect you through fear. They didn't know about my fighting prowess, my past reputation, or anything like that. If I'd been alone, they would have probably thought of me as a runt of a cripple having a laugh. But one look at two great big black Dobermans and they knew I meant business.

One of the dealers on the other side of the road, who wised up the situation very quickly, called me over and handed me some gear.

'Here,' he said. 'Try this. I like the way you operate. Come and meet a friend of mine.'

And that's how I got to know Frank Driscoll and we became good friends. He promised to set me up with as much puff as I could handle. As I went into the White House, I could hear the guys in the street asking, 'Who's that?'

'Says his name's Duchy,' replied the bloke I'd been talking to. 'He's a new shopper in town.'

After Frank and I had our meeting, I left the house only to find all these kids sitting on me motor.

'Oi, you fucking lot,' I shouted as I raised one of my crutches and the dogs started to growl. 'Get off my fucking car.' They scarpered. And, as I drove the Jag away, I wound down the window and shouted, 'Don't any of you lot think you can fuck with Duchy.' I'd made my point.

Back in Brockley Rise, I realised I needed to work out of a 'spill' – a place that sells illicit drugs and booze – and found one in Upper Brockley Road. It was a large garage which belonged to two brothers, and was an ideal outlet for selling my gear. Naturally, the guys who ran it got a cut of the business. I used to go there on Friday nights, sit there all night and sell the gear. Or else I'd go to the Golden Anchor pub and do the same.

It was all right until two so-called 'hard men', the Ford brothers, got out of prison and decided to make life a bit unbearable for people around there. They began drinking in the spill and wanted a cut of the gear and the money. Well, that was a useless idea because it would have left me with no fucking profit, so something had to give.

The Fords were trying to put the frighteners on everyone by way of a top guy called Steve who was an ex-villain with the big boys upstairs. I got on alright with Steve but he wanted to take over my gear business, which would have left me with nothing.

Some friends of the Fords disrespected me one evening when I was in the Golden Anchor. They were mouthing off about this, that and everything and thinking they were being funny. But, in fact, they were taking the piss. At the time, I had met a very good boxer named Chris.

I said to the idiots in the pub, 'OK, fair enough. You've disrespected me and now I'm going to show you something.'

With that, I went up to Chris's house and got him to come down to the pub and help me sort those two out.

I'd never seen anyone fight like Chris. He was a boxer and he was elegant. Bop, bop, bop, he would go and they'd fall down like nine-pins. Of course, the two guys we flattened went running to the Ford brothers who weren't too happy and decided to put their foot down. Intimidation was their game. They were in the spill all the time trying to nick my gear under the guise of protection.

'I don't need no fucking protection,' I told one of the brothers one night. 'I can look after my business myself. I always have and I always will.'

But they were having none of it and kept goading me until it kicked off. I whopped one of the brothers so severely he left the spill and said he was going to get his other brother and they would come back and shoot me.

'Don't push your luck, mate,' I said.

There was only one thing for me to do. I went back home to get my own gun. I got in touch with Craig Walters and he picked up his piece and we both went back with our guns.

The Ford brothers had got there before us, and seeing that I wasn't around to shoot, they decided to beat up another geezer severely and then leave. I wanted to go after them but some of my mates implored me to leave it alone.

That was the beginning of one of the craziest times of my life. Everything and everybody seemed to be spinning out of control.

One of the Ford brothers threatened me in the street the following day. He was with a guy who just went under the name of Mr Green, like someone out of a fucking Tarantino film. Then I heard that Steve, the Ford brothers' muscle, had been stabbed and was near death over in a block of flats on the estate. He had only just got out of prison and, for someone to weigh him up that quickly, things must have been bad. I thought, What the fuck's going on? I'd better slow down.

But things didn't slow down. I was working on an adventure playground with a friend of mine named Terry. Well, actually, we were there to make sure the kids didn't burn the place down really, when this kid came up and threatened Terry with a machete for no apparent reason. I quickly disarmed him, only for the kid to start shouting, 'Give me back me machete. It belongs to me dad.'

'And who is your dad, you little cunt?'

'My dad's Mr Green.'

I thought, Oh no, the mysterious Mr Green again.

Then, a couple of days later, I heard that my cousin Trevor Rooms had been shot dead.

He had been out for the night with friends at the local club, Champs, run by one of the top men, Del Woods. And the word was that Del Woods had shot Trevor during a dispute over something. So me and Craig decided we had better go down the club and find out exactly who this Del Woods was.

I casually mentioned to Michelle that we were going down Deptford to check on this Woods guy when she said, 'Del Woods? Oh, he goes out with a friend of mine named Sarah.'

I couldn't believe it. I thought I was caught up in some sort of crazy film. But it was going to get a lot crazier. Sharon vouched that Del had had nothing to do with Trevor's killing and that, although it had happened up the side of Del's club, it was someone else who had pulled the trigger.

I insisted on going to see Del. I might not have thought much of my family but I didn't like the fact that one of them had been mown down in South London.

I met Del in the luxurious offices at his club. He was every inch a gentleman and convinced me that he had had nothing to do with Trevor's death. Trevor had been mixed up with another mob altogether and Del promised to find out exactly who had ordered him shot.

Del and I became good friends. He was big-time. One of the reasons I was having trouble with people like Sammy and the Ford brothers was because I didn't have any sort of reputation when I first came south of the river. There was no respect for me like there had been in the East End because no one really knew who I was. But, once my friendship with Del Woods was established, that changed dramatically. I started training with Del and going down to his club. In fact, all of my firm did.

One night, Del said to me, 'I want to introduce you to a friend of mine.' And that's how I met a very smartly dressed, heavy-set guy named Tommy Smith.

I'd never seen this geezer before but I'd heard the name. The word was, it was Smith who had served up Steve. And his first words to me were, 'Hello, Duchy ... I've been paid to cut you up.'

It totally threw me. 'What did you say?' I managed to blurt out.

'Steady, Duchy,' said Del. 'Let Tommy explain.'

'You heard me, Duch,' Tommy continued. 'People have shelled out plenty of money to have you sliced. You must have been treading on too many toes.'

I looked at Del and then back at Tommy. What was going on?

Then Tommy let out a big belly laugh. 'But don't worry, I ain't going to carry it out,' he said. 'Del here has vouched for you. Says you're an all right bloke.'

'Pleased to hear it,' I muttered. 'So who set me up?'

'Guess.'

'The Ford brothers?'

'No. A guy named Mr Green.'

'The bastard,' I mumbled.

Then Del explained that Mr Green had been bearing a grudge ever since Chris the boxer and I had had a fight with two of his firm. He was also responsible for sending the kids with the machete to the adventure playground.

I knew Tommy wasn't joking if he had already served up the Ford brothers' muscle, Steve, on Del's instructions.

'The thing is, Duchy, Mr Green and the Ford brothers thought it was you who had ordered Steve to be cut,' continued Del. 'So, being the idiots they are, they thought they'd get Tommy to do the same to you. Fortunately, Tommy's my man, not Mr Green's, and he came right to me and told me.'

'Well, bugger me!' was all I could say. 'Excuse me, I've got some business to take care of.'

I hunted down Mr Green and his little firm, including the blokes Chris and I had fought with, and, with the help of Eugene, Craig and the boys, we weighed them off severely – very severely. They were no longer seen in the area after that.

With Del now a good friend, Mark Richardson and his dad Charlie still mates, Barry Adams looking out for me, and George Cauana's daughter as my girlfriend, I knew I was finally getting somewhere.

So that night, I splashed out on a bottle of champagne for me and Michelle.

'Hello, babes,' I said when I got home. 'Tonight we are going to celebrate.'

But, instead of being happy, Michelle just looked crestfallen. 'Who's told you?' she said annoyed. 'Who's spoiled my surprise?'

'Who's told me what, gorgeous?'

'Don't pretend, Duchy,' she said, miffed. 'You're no good at it.'

'I honestly don't know what you are talking about.'

'Yes you do. Someone's already told you, haven't they? Someone's already told you that I'm having your baby.'

9

Swings ... and Roundabouts

I SCREAMED FOR joy when Michelle's words finally sank in. We were having a baby ... *We were having a baby*! It hadn't been an accident. I'd built a very good relationship with 'Chelle, and we had both decided we wanted kids and had been trying for some time.

I don't know whether Michelle's mum actually approved because, when I told her that we wanted to start a family, she just looked me up and down and then looked away. Her dad didn't comment either. But then George had never really liked me because of my friendship with the Richardsons and former members of the Kray firm.

But the people who were dead set against the idea of me becoming a dad were the Social Services. When 'Chelle moved in with me in Barville Close, I remember one of them saying to me, 'I hear you've got a girlfriend now, Duchy ... well, remember to use condoms. A baby won't be any good for a man in your position.'

If anything, that made me want a child more. Social Services had been trying to run my life ever since I was born and now they thought they could tell me whether to raise a family or not. I'd show them.

The bubbly tasted even better that night as we toasted most of our friends, and especially the unborn child.

I was in a frenzy for a few days after the news and went round and told all my mates. Del Woods was especially pleased for me, and he had also found out what had really happened to my cousin Trevor.

Sitting down in the office of his club, he told me, 'It looks like it was a tragic mistake, Duchy. It seems a girl and this guy named Taylor McFurey were arguing outside the club when the girl's boyfriend came up and things got even more heated. The boyfriend pulled out a shooter and squeezed it at McFurey but he missed and hit Trevor by pure accident. I'm sorry, Duch, but that seems to have been the way it happened.'

I was saddened but at least I knew the truth. The guy was later banged up for the shooting.

One of the reasons I had been to see Del was to find a bit of extra work. With a baby on the way, alarm bells had started ringing. I needed a lot more money for baby clothes and food and one thing and another. But Del couldn't really help. He had already got enough people working for him like Laurence and Billy, down to Georgie and Uncle Bren, God rest his soul. And he was going through a slim time. 'But, if anything crops up, you'll be the first to know, Duchy,' he assured me.

Frankly, that wasn't going to buy nappies and toys and romper suits and fucking Heinz baby food, though, was it? But I kept all my money fears from Michelle. I didn't want to burden her with anything like that. So I went around as if there were no problems and started getting the flat ship-shape for when the baby was due.

The sales of puff were going OK but it was extra money I needed, so I decided to pull one of the old insurance scams by hustling this guy I'd met down the local pub.

He was a genuinely decent guy who lived on the estate and he got to know me and Eugene and the rest of the boys. We became friends and would go round his flat where he had this fantastic top-of-the-range hi-fi system and lots of other electronic stuff. He was really into music and was always keen for me to go round there with my guitar and sing a few songs that I'd written.

One day round the pub, I mentioned to him, 'How would you like to make a bit of money?'

'Depends. How?'

'You got any contents insurance on your flat?'

'Yeah.'

'Well, you're sorted then, ain't ya?'

'What do you mean, Duchy?'

And then I explained to him that I'd organise a little break-in at his flat and take all his valuable electronics equipment – video, hi-fi, televisions and all that – and he could just claim it all back from the insurance company.

Then, when he got the cheque for several thousand pounds from the insurance people, we'd split it and I'd give him back all his equipment.

That way, we both made out of it and nobody lost – except the fucking insurance company and they didn't count anyway.

'No one will know the burglary was set up, I promise you,' I said as way of assurance. 'I'm an expert when it comes to all sorts of things and especially theft from houses.'

But the guy was not completely convinced, even though I

could see he was tempted when I pointed out how much profit he'd make.

'Nah, I don't think so, Duch, I'm not really into all that. Let's just leave it, shall we?' was his reply.

But I couldn't leave it. I had a baby coming in a few months' time and I needed a bit of money stashed away; a few thousand would be well handy.

I brooded over what to do for a few days and then decided I'd go ahead with it anyway.

So I told the guy, 'You're probably right. Why risk it, eh? I don't know what came over me. Let's forget about it altogether. Want another drink?'

And so, to all intents and purposes, the plan was shelved and things went back to normal.

One day, I went down his flat with my guitar and talked my way in. The bloke said he would have to go out for an hour and I told him not to worry, that I would look after things while he was away.

As soon as he left, I phoned my boys and we emptied the place in double-quick time.

Obviously, the guy who lived there knew who had done it but I was banking on him going along with the insurance scam and keeping quiet. I was willing to smash the door up a bit to make it look like a break-in.

But he was having none of it. Next time I saw him, he said, 'All right, Duchy, I know it was you and your mates who did me over. Now just give me my stuff back and that'll be the end of it.'

But I had no intention of giving him anything back. 'Can't do that,' I said. 'Otherwise I won't make anything out of it.'

'I'm warning you, Duchy, give me back my stuff or I'm going to the police.'

So I shouted at him, 'You're not getting your stuff back. You want to be a grass, you be a fucking grass and see where it gets ya. You'll be weighed in as a grass, now I'm warning you.'

So what did he do? He went to the Old Bill.

The knock on the door came one night while I was sitting with 'Chelle. I wasn't fearing it because I knew it was pretty inevitable and I'd got rid of all the gear in an afternoon.

It wasn't the knock on the door that troubled me or even the opening phrase, 'Hello, Duchy, you're about to be nicked, son.' It was the sad look in Michelle's eyes. She just looked at me and it was as if every ounce of happiness just drained out of her. She didn't even say anything, she just looked. And she looked so dejected.

She was going to have her first baby and I had left her in the lurch. She just looked at me as if to say, 'How could you be so thoughtless, so stupid?' And I didn't know the answer to that. I'd been trying to provide for my child's future. That's how I saw it.

With my record, I was quickly sentenced to six months banged up in Feltham.

Clat ... clat ... clat ... clat ...

I felt like shit because of what I'd done. I'd got myself into trouble and left my family out there to fend for themselves. And, with the reputation I had, if someone couldn't hurt me there was a good chance they would try to hurt my family. So I had to warn 'Chelle, 'Don't do this, don't do that ... they could hurt you.'

Even though the Scrubs was like my kingdom and I ran my wing, I still felt terrible for having got myself in there. But the thing was not to brood on it, just get on with it and get it over with. I'd learned a lot from those old days in Lewes when Charlie Richardson used to run the nick. I'd learned how to be the 'daddy' of whatever wing I was on, in whatever prison I went to. The Scrubs was no different. The screws treated me OK because they knew I had the power to handle the rest of the cons and get them to do as they were told.

Again, I wasn't allowed a guitar in the Scrubs, but I used to sing in my cell anyway, and even here the screws would say, 'You know, Duchy, lad, you should take that up professionally, forget all this villainy. You could be a star, mate.'

I'd usually reply, 'Bollocks.'

Michelle somehow forgave me for what I had done and used to come and visit me in prison as often as she could. I don't know how she got there but she did, even when she was very heavily pregnant.

But I saw myself as scum. I wasn't proud of anything I had done or how I had got to where I was. My kid was soon to be born and I wasn't going to be there for it. How would any dad feel?

I used to go down the gym at the nick and work out in a burst of rage. I'd weight-lift and bench-press until my muscles couldn't take any more. I was trying to punish myself for all the stupid things that I'd done in my life. The screws kept a tight eye on me. They must have sensed there were demons in my head and they didn't want to see me go over the top.

One day, one of them came up to me in the gym and said, 'Duchy, I've been watching you bench-press and you know you are pushing more than most people do on the TV in those competitions.'

I just stared and said nothing.

But he meant what he'd said and went to have a word with the Governor.

Next time I was in the gym, the screw came up to me again.

'You know, Duchy, you've got a good missus, you've got a baby on the way and you've got a life,' he said. 'I've had a word with the Guv about you and he wants to give you a chance. But you fuck it up like, and you're finished.'

My ears pricked up.

He continued, 'If we give you the security to go out of prison and weight-lift for your country, would you be interested?'

I didn't have to think long. They were giving me the chance to get out of prison once a week and represent Great Britain weight-lifting against able-bodied people.

'S'pose so,' I said.

And that was the beginning of anyone taking me seriously about anything in my life. I didn't want the screws to know it, but I wasn't going to let them down.

I started benching 95kg which is not very impressive, but others were only doing 75kg. Then, as I started eating properly, sleeping properly and training regularly, I moved over 100kg and the next thing I knew I could bench-press 150kg, which was three times my body weight. There was no one in Great Britain who could beat me bench-pressing at my weight. I would compete in different places all over the country and win a stack of medals. And, remember, this was all against able-bodied lifters.

For once, I started behaving meself in the nick. No more fighting with the screws. I didn't want to jeopardise getting out of there and going home to my girl.

And then, one day, the news came. 'Duchy,' said one of the kangas. 'Your Miss has gone into labour.'

That was it, I was already packing me stuff.

'Now steady on, son,' he continued. 'We are going to give you a 24-hour leave starting from tomorrow.

'But I want to go now.'

'Well, you can't.'

'And, anyway, I don't want no 24 hours. What do you

expect me to do, run down there, kiss 'Chelle and fuck off?'

So, by a miracle, they decided that, because I'd been behaving myself on the days I was allowed out weight-lifting, this time they'd give me 48 hours.

By the time I got to the hospital, the baby had already been born, but it didn't matter. It was a beautiful little baby boy who weighed 7lb 6oz and we named him Duch Junior, although everyone immediately called him DJ.

Michelle's mum turned up, and so did my mum and dad.

'Is the child all right ... is the child all right?' demanded my father, the Rev Jeff Peter.

'Of course he's all right, Dad,' I said. 'Look, count 'em, ten tiny fingers, ten tiny toes. Two perfect legs. What were you expecting? For him to look like his old man?' I sneered.

We were seeing more and more of my mum and dad because we used to go down to Forest Hill for Sunday lunch or over to Michelle's mum who was still living in Brixton. We were really trying to make a go of being a family unit.

But my father was always aloof. He had never approved of me because I wouldn't abide by his rules, and because every time he saw me it must have reminded him of what he did to me at birth.

'Look, Dad, the baby's fine. We won't have to give this one away,' I smirked.

And, as soon as I said it, I could have cut my tongue out. Tears welled up in my mum's eyes and Dad just glared at me.

'You don't know what you're talking about, son,' he said and turned on his heel to leave the ward. 'You don't know the half of it.'

'What half?' I said. Then I turned to Mum. 'I'm sorry, Mum,' I explained. 'I didn't mean to say anything, I didn't mean to hurt you. But you know what it's like between Dad and me.'

'Let it drop, son, let it drop.'

And that's what I did … for the time being. But one day, one day, I was going to get an explanation.

I held DJ, my son, stayed a night and then I had to go back to prison. After seeing DJ, I realised that the only thing I wanted to do was to get out of the nick and get on with my life.

The days dragged by, but every week 'Chelle would come and see me and she'd bring DJ with her.

Because I had quite a bit of standing in the Scrubs, my visits were different. There would be one visiting table for me, my missus and my baby. And everyone else would be crammed on little tables. The other cons would go, 'How come he's sitting over there like lord of the fucking manor?' And the screws would reply, 'That's Duchy.' But no amount of special treatment could make up for the fact that I was inside while my son was outside waiting for me. But I finished my bird a few weeks after DJ was born and I swore to myself that this time I'd go straight and everything was going to be all right.

And I tried, and I did go straight.

I'd been in and out of prison all my life but I still suffered from that culture shock that all cons get when they walk back into freedom. Just the feeling of being able to go to bed when you want, go for a walk when you want, buy what you want, is amazing.

The first couple of months were bliss. I was chilling out with the boys, smoking a bit of puff, and not really working. But Michelle and I were happy. I'd feel proud taking DJ out in the pram, even if it was only over the park. Things, I thought, can't get much better than this. I even went down Social Services to see if they could get me a proper job. I was going to take being a dad seriously.

Then, one day, I was down in Peckham, South London, and I bumped into a really old friend of mine, literally bumped into her on the street.

'Mind where the fuck you're going,' I said. And then I glanced up. 'Rhona! It is you, innit?'

'Duchy. Yeah, course it's me.'

'How have you been?'

'I was just about to say the same.'

'Well, well, well.'

Then there was a silent pause.

'Fancy a drink?' we both said at the same time.

And that's how I renewed my friendship with Rhona. I'd first met her in Prince's Lodge back in Limehouse. She used to sit in my room there at night and listen to me playing guitar and singing. She was gorgeous, everyone knew her and everyone liked her. But she was only a mate, because she had a boyfriend named Paddy at the time.

We got talking in the pub and she told me that she was a single mum now and had two small kids. Paddy, she said, was ancient history.

'That's funny,' I said. 'I've just become a dad. Great, innit?'

'Not when you're on your own and you've got two of them yelling and screaming all day long.'

'No, I s'pose not.'

'Don't worry, Duchy, you've got it all to come.'

So I renewed my friendship with Rhona and she became friends with Michelle, and would even do a spot of babysitting if we wanted to go out for the evening.

To this day, I don't know why it happened, but women have always been one of my great weaknesses.

I'd popped down to Rhona's house one night to do a little job for her, help her put up some shelves or something. Next thing I know, we're having a bottle of wine together and having a laugh about the old times.

'I always fancied you, Rhona, when we were back in Prince's Lodge,' I said. 'But I didn't like the look of your boyfriend Paddy, a big bruiser.'

'It weren't him you was supposed to sleep with, Duchy,' she giggled, and poured another drink.

'You mean …'

'Well, you ain't too bad yourself. And I've always liked a man with muscles.'

So one thing led to another and, before I knew it, I was in bed with her.

The first thing I heard was the doorbell ringing. I stirred from sleep and then realised it was early morning. 'Christ, who can that be?' But, before the words were out of my mouth, I knew it wasn't the fucking milkman.

And then I heard Michelle's voice. She was talking to one of Rhona's kids.

'Is your mummy in?' she said.

'Upstairs.'

And as I heard the feet on the stairs I realised I was done for this time.

Michelle shouted as she continued to climb the stairs, 'Rhona, Rhona, you up there?'

Then there was the knock on the door. I was completely powerless to do anything. The door swung open.

'Rhona, you don't know where …' Michelle stared, her eyes wide, her mouth open, '… Duchy is, do you?'

There was a split-second of silence then Rhona jumped out of bed and started shouting, 'If you want your man, you'll have to fight for him,' she said.

Michelle gave her a withering look and shouted directly at me, 'Are you coming home?'

I was out of bed by that time and trying to put my trousers on, which, as you can imagine, was difficult at the best of times. But I managed it.

'Duchy, come back here,' said Rhona.

But I was off. I got in the car. Michelle snatched the keys from me.

'I'll drive,' she said. 'You've got explaining to do.'

I told 'Chelle that it was a complete one-off and that I'd had the opportunity and I took it. I told her how sorry I was. I told her how it wouldn't happen again.

'And how do you think I feel?' she said. 'You've betrayed me, Duchy. I've been up all night worried sick that you'd maybe had an accident in the car or something … but I should have known … you were with that filthy scrubber I thought was my friend. How could you do it to me, Duchy, how could you do it?'

So I told her again how sorry I was, told her how it would never happen again. And then, trying to calm things down, I said, 'How's DJ?'

'As if you bloody well care,' she replied as she pushed her foot flat down on the accelerator.

And that's what really hurt me.

It took a long time for 'Chelle to forgive me and begin to trust me again. In fact, she sorted out her differences with Rhona quicker than she did with me. I was left there to hang on and to squirm while Rhona said she was sorry and everything was smoothed over eventually. But then that's the way with women. If it had been the other way round and I had caught Michelle sleeping with another geezer, well, I suppose I would have administered a severe beating and never wanted to lay eyes on him again. But it's different with women.

I wasn't happy about what I had done and so I decided to put all my energy into the weight-lifting and try to blot things out. I was so good at bench-pressing by this time that I was being selected to represent Great Britain in overseas competitions.

One of my major triumphs – my last one, in fact – was in Thun in Switzerland. But I almost didn't go. All the competitors who'd been invited there had to find their own air fares. Some of them got the money from local businesses, paid themselves or got it from sponsorship. But I had no one.

So I said to the British officials, 'I'm not going unless I get a ticket, because I just can't afford it.'

'I'm sorry,' they told me, 'but we don't do that. You'll have to get some sponsorship.'

'But I'm the best hope you've got, you know that. Oh, and by the way, I'll need some spending money.'

They eventually relented and paid for my trip.

But it was trouble right from the beginning because there was another disabled geezer, also a weight-lifter from East London, who had a hard side like me. And for the whole two weeks, all he went on about was, 'You've been in trouble, ain'tcha? You've been in prison … you've been in prison.' He started getting right up my nose.

He was in my face all the time, going on about how much bird I'd done, and that I thought I was hard, and that he had heard about me in East London. I felt like dropping the bloody weights on his head. The worst thing was that I had to share a room with this tosser and another bloke.

Anyway, the Championships started and the British team was doing very badly, we weren't anywhere in sight of the medals.

The bloke from the East End had been taunting me and I was blaming him for putting me off. But then I thought, Bollocks, I'll show them.

I don't know where I got the energy from, but suddenly I

was pushing big weights. The rest of the team was urging me on. I was the last hope left.

'C'mon, Duchy,' they were shouting. 'C'mon, mate.'

The next thing I knew, I was in the medals table and they were putting a silver around my neck. I felt so proud standing there. I'd won a silver medal for my country. None of the rest of the team brought back anything, although they had tried their hardest. They were all congratulating me and we were having a right old time.

At the banquet afterwards, I started drinking lots of vodka with the Polish team which turned out to be a bad move because when I drink vodka I forget and I get out of hand.

I staggered back to my hotel room and noticed there was a book lying on my bed. I picked it up and said, 'Whose book's this?' or something like that.

Next thing I know, the East End guy jumps up in bed and goes, 'What's all this shouting, you fucking moron, coming in here waking me up.'

'Steady on,' I replied. 'It's banquet night and I won. What do you want to go to bed for? Everyone is out there laughing and drinking and enjoying themselves. And you, you miserable cunt, are in bed shouting at me.'

Then he said the magic words that were guaranteed to cause him a lot of pain and suffering: 'Fuck off, you black bastard.'

I replied, 'You call me that again and I'll knock you out.'

'Black Bastard.'

And that was it. I connected one straight on his nose as hard as I could. He fell back into the pillow, blood everywhere. I picked him up by the shoulders and was just about to nut him when he burst out crying.

At that, the other roommate started running down the hall shouting for help and complete pandemonium broke out.

Back in Britain, I was hauled up before the committee and

banned from appearing in future competitions for 12 months. Not bad for the only person who had brought a medal back from Switzerland.I went on to win all the freestyle championships for two years running and my martial arts became a big part of my life and still is. Although I'd always been pretty nimble with my *nunchukas*, I'd never really been trained.

It was Eugene's idea to begin with. One day he said, 'You know what? I'm gonna get graded. I'm gonna join a Tae Kwon Do club and get graded.'

My mate, Paul, told me about a guy called Freddy Steadman who was – and still is – one of the best fighters in south east London. They tried everything with Freddy, but he just kept knocking them down. When I met Fred and started training with him, I was shocked to see that he only had one leg and, despite this, everyone was still shit-scared of him. I have learned a lot about pride and self-respect from Fred and whenever we trained I would see that look of determination in his eyes. When he told me how he lost his leg, I could understand why ...

He was at home with his family one day when there was a knock at the door. With his little boy in tow, Fred went to answer it. He opened the door and was met by a man with a shotgun. Without a second thought, the man fired the gun – thankfully missing Fred's little boy – and hitting Fred in the leg.

When Fred told me this story, I remember that, instead of feeling sorry for him, I felt stronger in myself and I knew that I was no longer alone. It spurred me on.

The trouble was, I didn't know where to start, so I got hold of one of my social workers, Martin Honeysett, and told him my idea. He got me a few leaflets and said, 'What kind of martial arts are you interested in, Duchy?'

'Well,' I replied. 'I was brought up by a Singaporean family and I'm OK with *nunchukas*. Now if you can find me a class for *nunchukas*, I'd be happy to go.'

The bloke only went and found one for me. He came back and told me the place to go to in Sydenham. The guys I had to see were Bob McCormack and Bob Chaproniere, who were in the national *nunchuka* team for Great Britain.

In order to get graded, I showed them how I could handle the martial arts weapons and straight away they wanted to give me a black. But Chaproniere said, 'No, I think we'll give you a brown or you won't have anything to work for.'

Michelle and I had patched up our differences since my fling with Rhona and I had started working more on my music. There was a girl on our estate who was also into music. Her name was Mica Paris, who would later go on to be a major star. She was dedicated to her singing and had a beautiful voice. We'd talk about music all the time and I'd play her a few things. One day, she introduced me to her best friend, who I'll call Debbie.

She was a beautiful girl, Debbie, and I had to keep telling myself, 'Don't, Duch. You've been in deep trouble this way once before. Don't let it happen again.' But I couldn't stop thinking about her and I'd make any excuse to chat with her.

One night, Rhona invited both me and Michelle down to her house.

'I can't go, 'Chelle,' I explained. 'It's me martial arts class tonight. Have you seen my *nunchukas* anywhere?'

'That's funny, you don't usually go on a Thursday, Duchy.'

'Nah, but this week it's been changed, 'cos Bob Chaproniere's having tomorrow off for a long weekend.'

'Oh, I see. OK then, I'll tell Rhona.'

So Michelle took DJ down to Rhona's while I ... went to

Debbie's. I feel like dog shit about all this now. But that's the way it was. I went to see her.

I pieced everything together later. It seems that Michelle and Rhona were watching telly and having a drink and 'Chelle decided to put DJ down in Rhona's other room. Things seemed fine, he was always a good-natured baby, never much trouble. He was placed on his back like you're supposed to do.

About 20 minutes later, Michelle went to check on DJ and found that he was blue.

'Rhona, Rhona,' she screamed, 'something's happened to DJ. He's gone blue. Call an ambulance. Now, now!'

Michelle was hysterical and frantic. 'Where's Duchy, where's Duchy when I need him?' and she burst into sobs.

The ambulance arrived in lightning-quick time and took DJ and 'Chelle to King's College Hospital in Denmark Hill, one of the busiest and best hospitals in London.

While all the drama was going on, I had this other girl on my mind – I was so full of shit!. That's when the doorbell rang. It was Rhona and she was furious.

'You might have been able to fool Michelle, but you couldn't fool me,' she screamed. 'Now get down to King's College Hospital, DJ is seriously ill.'

I jumped in a car with Rhona and a friend and we drove over to Denmark Hill as fast as we could but, throughout the journey, I had this awful feeling in the pit of my stomach that something was severely wrong.

I raced into the hospital, cursing the slowness of my artificial legs and crutches.

'Mr Peter … my wife's brought our baby in … her name's Michelle … I've got to see them,' I blurted out, barely able to breathe.

'Through here, sir.'

And, as I went through the swing doors into a small room, all my fears were realised. There was Michelle cradling DJ in her arms and sobbing, sobbing, sobbing, 'My baby's dead, my baby's dead.'

I held them both as tears trickled down my face.

The hospital had done everything they could but DJ had died at just five months old. It was a cot death due to a viral infection. It smashed to pieces my relationship with Michelle – and I was just as much to blame.

Studies on the role of viral and bacterial infection in cot death are still continuing to this day, but nothing could ease our pain then, and it never will.

At the time, I felt like the worst person on God's earth for what I had been up to. I'd cheated on Michelle once again, and when she needed me I was in some other bird's house talking bollocks. My mind was nowhere near the protection of my child that night, where it should have been, and I blame myself to this day.

Michelle was totally distraught and I feared for both her health and her sanity. She cried and cried for weeks and, even to this day, she can't go up to the grave where DJ is buried in Grove Park Cemetery, South London.

My mind was also shot through and I even thought about suicide, but instead I did the one thing I always did when I wanted to blot out reality, I started drinking heavily and taking drugs.

I was on a deep, dark, downward spiral.

I'd get up in the morning unable to remember what I had done the night before. I remember having to get the money together to get a family plot in the cemetery because over and over in my mind there was a waking nightmare that they were going to dig up an old grave and put my baby on top of someone else.

I'd wake up in the night covered in sweat, and during the day I'd stumble around after drinking a bottle of good Polish vodka for breakfast.

Whatever villainy I got up to, I can't remember, and that's the honest truth, but even my mates in the old firm would take me to one side and try to get me to ease up.

'You've got to relax a bit, Duchy,' Eugene would implore. 'Take it easy, mate, you're being too hard on yourself.'

I was smoking shedloads of puff at the time, but even that couldn't get me to relax.

'Ease up ... EASE UP! What the fuck do you know about it, Eugene?' I'd bark back. 'It's not your child that's dead.'

And then I'd be off on another bender. I'd break into houses and steal things while I was high and drunk. I'd do anything and take anything that could make me a few bob. A few bob that would help me get that plot in the cemetery, a family plot where we could all lie. A few bob that would help me get another bottle of vodka.

A few bob for this, a few bob for that, a few bob for ... And then, one day, I took a look at myself in the mirror.

It wasn't a pretty sight. The big fucking hard gangster – I don't think.

I had to do something and, in my fucked-up, addled brain, I thought that running away might do the trick. If I could just get away from Brockley, things would be all right. There had been other child deaths in our small community in Barville Close. My mate George's kid Charlie had been killed when an empty Christmas hamper fell on him and suffocated him, and a few months before DJ died there had been another cot death. Three children dead in a space of months. I blamed the area, I blamed everything.

There was no communication at all between Michelle and

me. There were no 'I love yous', no 'Let's try agains'. There was nothing.

But I couldn't just walk away. If I did, it would be like saying to myself that DJ had never existed, that his five months of life had never happened. I wasn't going to have that. I wanted to keep his memory and his love alive.

And that's when, for the first time in months, I picked up my guitar.

And with tears rolling down my face, I wrote a song for my son called 'When I Cry'.

It was the turning point in my life.

When I had finished writing it, I knew there had to be a future, and that, God willing, I was going to grasp that future.

I was reminded of what the screws had told me when I was down in the Scrubs, that I ought to take up singing and songwriting professionally. But I knew that if I confided my dream to anyone they would only laugh. After all, I was Duchy, I was a villain, I was all mouth.

But I played the song to Michelle and, for the first time in months, the pain seemed to ease from her face.

'That's lovely, Duchy,' she said. 'And you've got such a lovely voice.'

And I decided there and then that, whether or not anyone believed in me, I was going to believe in myself. I was going to try and live my dream and be a singer-songwriter.

I knew there were bound to be lots of setbacks on the road. And after all, when you've been a villain all your life, it's very difficult to change. I wasn't going to become an angel overnight.

But I had a chance – admittedly a slim chance, but a chance, a fighting chance – to try and make something out of my life.

10

Music Man

THE DEATH OF DJ totally destroyed my relationship with Michelle. I couldn't get any sense out of her. I'd ask, 'Do you love me?'

And she'd reply, 'I don't know. I don't know what I feel for you any more.'

We discussed our problems with a doctor who was an expert in the kind of upheaval we had been through. And his reponse was devastating. 'It can take a mother up to ten years to get over a cot death,' he told us. 'And you, Duch, it'll probably take you as long as five years to recover properly.'

Although DJ's death hadn't been my fault, the events surrounding it continued to haunt me. If I hadn't been fucking around, maybe I could have done something sooner. I was plagued by the idea that Michelle's attitude had more to do with my repeated unfaithfulness than it did with the death of our son. Of course, I was wrong. Like any mother would have been, she was totally shell-shocked by the loss of DJ.

I did everything I could, legally and illegally, to get the money for the burial plot in Grove Park Cemetery, South London. And then I'd ask Michelle, 'How do you feel? Why don't you come up to the grave with me? It's nice and peaceful.'

But she refused to go, so I'd always have to make the journey on my own, which made me feel even more isolated. We were drifting apart and it seemed to be happening in slow motion with neither of us able to stop it.

My first reaction had been to try for another baby as quickly as possible. But it doesn't work like that. If you desperately try to have a child, things don't seem to happen. It might have been because of all the tension and the strain, but Michelle couldn't get pregnant. And then there was Michelle's rejection of me – I was noticing that more and more.

Still, I was determined somehow to establish myself as a musician and I thought, in some naïve way, that by doing so I would rehabilitate myself in Michelle's eyes.

My days consisted of selling some gear in the pubs round where I lived and then going up to Central London to busk around the Tube stations and make a bit more money. I was still able to get good deals from the guys down in Brixton but the days when we could knock out as much puff as we wanted in the old 'spill' were gone. The death of DJ had left me without all the enthusiasm I had when I used to run the firm.

In many ways, I was back to square one. But at least it was on my own terms. I was determined that music would be the number-one priority in my life. But, unfortunately, to pursue that I needed money, and the only way I could make money was by selling gear.

The busking was fairly lucrative as well, and I enjoyed it. I could make about seven quid in half-an-hour, which wasn't bad in the mid-Eighties.

I used to choose one song and sing it from the beginning to the middle. There was no point in singing the whole song because if anyone had given money they would have already passed by. So I'd start again with the verse and chorus. If you played the whole lot every time, you'd wear yourself out.

Obviously, when busking you have to perform well-known hits in order to get some response. But now and again, I'd slip in one of my own songs, one I had been working on.

They usually went down quite well which made me feel good. I also liked singing them because the acoustics are so good down in the Tube station, and that way I could judge what the song would be like if it was well produced.

Many times I would get moved along by London Transport officials but I was never arrested or anything like that. And I used to get quite a kick when Japanese tourists came by. They would inevitably stop to take a picture of me. And they'd chatter, 'Blitish pop star, Blitish pop star,' then giggle as they moved on.

Piccadilly or London Bridge were the best places to earn a few bob because they were always crowded. Sometimes I would pretend I was waiting for a train which was all right as long as the guards didn't see a hat, and I used to get a buzz hearing the trains rush into the station and my voice disappearing, only for it to come back as the train started on its journey through another tunnel.

Another favourite place for busking was 'Cardboard City', this huge place near Waterloo Station where the homeless lived. It became such a famous place that it turned into a tourist attraction and the well-heeled would go down there either to give to their less fortunate brethren or to gawp at them. Whichever way, a good pitch there could earn me quite a bit of money.

But I was under no illusions. I never thought that some rock star manager would suddenly happen upon me in Cardboard City and say to his colleagues, 'Jeez, I just heard this black cripple kid who sings like an angel. We must sign him up.'

I was happy just to play my music, like I always had done.

In the old days, me and Mica Paris used to sing together in the front room of her mate's house. 'You're going to be a star one day, Duchy,' she'd tell me.

'Nah, you'll get there first,' I'd reply. 'You've got a wonderful voice.'

And Mica wasn't the only star to come out of the estate in Brockley Rise. There was Maxi Priest, or Max Elliot as he was to me, whose silky-smooth voice earned him the nickname 'King of Lover's Rock'. He became a good friend of mine after hearing me sing in the Community Hall at a leaving party for a guy from the adventure playground. And footballer Ian Wright was also from Brockley Rise, so there was plenty of talent about.

But I'd go home to the flat in Brockley and then the weight of the world would come down on us again. And after a while, I realised that me and Michelle would probably have to get out of there. Even though we were going through a bad patch, we were trying to keep our relationship on track.

I remember saying to 'Chelle that I thought we would be doing the right thing by getting out of Brockley. I told her that I'd been down to the council and begged them to re-house us after all that had happened.

Some time later, they came back with an offer for us – a

flat in Henry Cooper Way, Mottingham, South London, not very far away and nearer to the cemetery where DJ was buried. We jumped at the chance and took it. As soon as we saw it, we knew it was perfect – it was very secluded, just what we were looking for. We were both really happy. We put our arms around each other and kissed – and this time she didn't back off.

Our daughter Jade was born in August 1986. But it was a turbulent time, with both of us trying our best to keep the relationship alive. Michelle was still rejecting me and I began to notice it more and more as we started on the road to separation. It was make or break time and, sadly, we decided that we both needed our own space to work things out.

A few months later, Michelle moved out only to tell me that she was pregnant again, which made my head spin. I tried to get back together with her, for the sake of the kids, but she said that I had to go back for both her and the kids, or not at all. By the time Michelle gave birth to my son Dean in February 1988, we had split up and I knew that it was going to be permanent. Michelle has always stuck by me as a friend and has been a wonderful mother to our children. And you can't say much better than that.

It was around this time that something really weird happened in the pub one evening. This guy came up to me and started looking at me really quizzically.

'Oi, what's your game, mate?' I said.

'Nothing.'

Then a couple of minutes later, he was back again.

'Excuse me, is your name Raymond?' he asked.

'Who wants to know?'

'I think I'm your step-brother, Steve.'

'I don't have any step-brothers.'

'Well, not actually your step-brother, but I'm, well, I'm Steve Coward. Ian and June are my mum and dad. I remember you when you were little. You used to live with us. Is your name Raymond? It *is* you, isn't it?'

I was totally taken aback. 'Of course it's me,' I said. 'How many other black brothers do you have with no legs?'

Ian and June Coward were living on the Isle of Sheppey, off the north Kent coast. They'd got a small farm there and June was breeding dogs. They had been the couple I'd always regarded as my 'real' parents. They were the ones who had given me my English accent.

I went down there with Steve as soon as I could. It was an emotional time because June had always regarded me as one of her own kids and I'd stayed with the family a lot longer than any other foster children.

June was misty-eyed and couldn't do enough for me, fussing round me like she had done when I was a child.

Ian showed me around the place and it was great because we both had an interest in dogs, although I diplomatically forgot to tell them about the days when I used to enter Chub into dog-fighting contests.

As Ian and I were rummaging around in an outhouse, he pulled out an old piece of wood with some wheels on it.

'Remember this, Raymond?' he said, holding it up.

'Erm … vaguely,' I replied.

'It's what's left of your trolley. I made it for you years ago so you could get around easier. That was before you had the operations on your legs, Ray.'

'Christ! Of course, I remember it now.'

'You loved that trolley and went everywhere on it. Now, without the sides, it looks more like a home-made skateboard. I don't know why I've kept it, I might as well throw it out.'

'No, don't do that … don't do that,' I said.

When it came to leave, we all agreed that we must stay in touch and that's one of the things we have managed to do.

Ian and June know all about my past, the violence and the times I've been in nick, but they have never been judgemental towards me. They still treat me as one of their family.

I know I should have asked June if she knew why my real parents had given me away at birth. But I didn't ask, and I doubt whether she would have known. I didn't ask because I didn't want June to think it was important to me. I'd tried to put it to the back of my mind.

Although I was doing all right singing by myself and selling gear, I used to remember fondly the old days back at school when Jools Holland and Glenn Tilbrook came and helped us record our charity EP. I wonder whatever happened to Paul Low and that group, Vine.

I was pulled out of my daydream in the pub by this guy who got talking to me. His name was Peter Allen and he also played guitar along with his brother Mark. So we started talking about music and he offered me a lift home in his clapped-out old Mini.

Back in Henry Cooper Way, I showed him my old guitar and started playing him some recent songs I had been working on. He was mightily impressed and there and then drove straight back to his place to pick up his guitar and returned within half-an-hour. We played together all night long, right until the sun came up.

I don't know how we decided on Harlequin for the name of the band we wanted to form, but it seemed right at the time. We soon got Peter's brother Mark to join and then we added a drummer named Gary and a guy named John on lead guitar.

We were all set.

'What do we do now then, Duch?' asked Peter.

'We ... er ... well, we get some gigs together, don't we?' I replied hopefully.

'How?'

'Good one, Peter, good one ...'

I knew he wasn't going to take this well, but I said, 'How about we go on *Opportunity Knocks*?'

There was silence.

'You're bloody joking. Like Lena fucking Zavaroni!'

'No listen, it's all changed now. There's a new show called *Bob Says Opportunity Knocks* with that comedian bloke, what's-his-name, Bob Monkhouse, and they are looking for people to audition. It's all in the back of *Melody Maker*. Have a look.' I handed him the weekly music paper.

'*Opportunity Bloody Knocks!*'

But Peter did have a look and, after his initial shock, thought it might be a good idea, or at least a laugh anyway.

So I sent off for the application forms which we filled in and sent back. And, within no time at all, we received a date for us to go and audition. It was in a studio in Hammersmith, West London.

I couldn't sleep the night before the audition and my biggest worry was whether I would break a string while I was playing. It kept going round and round in my mind.

The next morning, Peter and I set off for Hammersmith. Although we had filled in the application form as a five-piece group, only two of us could make it.

But we had rehearsed the song we were going to perform, 'I Can Hear the Children Crying', as a duo so we weren't that worried.

The floor manager, or whatever he was called, was the first person to approach us.

'Name?'

'Harlequin,' I said. 'But ...'

'But what?'

'But there's only two of us. You see, Mark couldn't make it 'cos he works as a train driver. Gary, well, Gary works for a bank ... and so does John so he couldn't get the time off. So there's just the two of us ... sir.'

'And your names are?'

'Peter and Duch Peter.'

'I see.'

But I could see he couldn't as he scratched his head. For all he knew, we might as well be the new Peters and Lee with the blind guy substituted by a cripple.

'Yes, well ...' said the floor manager. 'Can I have your CD then?'

Peter and I looked at each other. 'We don't have a CD,' I stammered. 'We thought if we could win *Opportunity Knocks* then someone might give us a record deal and then we'd make a CD. That's what we thought.'

The floor manager was getting more frustrated. 'No,' he said very slowly as if talking to a child, 'I mean the CD that contains the backing music for the song you are going to perform.' And he looked down his clipboard. '"I Can Hear the Children Crying" ... Do you have the CD?'

'We don't have one,' I replied with a weak smile.

'You don't have one?'

'No, like, we play our guitars and sing. That's all.' I let out a little stifled laugh.

'You play your guitars and sing,' he said by way of verification. 'Well, best of luck,' and with raised eyebrows he turned and walked away.

Then we looked around at who else would be auditioning. Not only had they probably got the Royal Fucking Philharmonic Orchestra on their backing CD they were all dressed up in stage costumes like a load of bloody trapeze artistes. We had our jeans on.

'Harlequin,' someone shouted and the next thing we knew, me and Peter stumbled on to the stage. I don't know what anyone thought when they saw two guitar players, one on crutches.

'In your own time.'

'One ... two ... one, two, three, four ...' We were away, and we were on a high.

The moment we started playing, the whole place went dead quiet. And as we hit the chorus on 'I Can Hear the Children Crying', I looked at Peter and we both winked. Everything seemed to come together at the right time.

As we finished the song, we were both beaming while the audience erupted into wild clapping. Then someone started stamping their feet, and then all of them started stamping.

Clat ... clat ... clat ... clat ... it sounded like marching. And then even louder – clat ... clat ... clat ... clat ... It was the sound of applause.

And, for just a few moments, I was able to drink it in. Backstage after the audition, Peter and me were still smiling. 'That went well,' said Peter.

'Not half,' I replied. 'And just with two guitars. Who needs fucking CD backing tapes anyway?'

And we burst out laughing, then went down the pub on our way home.

Two days later, we got a letter from the show's organisers congratulating us and telling us that we had been picked to appear on *Bob Says Opportunity Knocks*.

Yes, yes, I thought. This is it, we're on our way. We were totally ecstatic.

Then a couple of days later, we got another letter, a very apologetic letter. It said that we couldn't go on *Opportunity*

Knocks because another band had already been picked from the London area, and we should never have been sent the earlier letter in the first place.

To say we were gutted is an understatement; it absolutely mortified the band. I even thought about getting me *nunchukas* out and going to see that bloody Bob Monkhouse. But, instead, I tried to cheer everyone up. 'Don't worry,' I said. 'We'll just get a record deal anyway.'

'How are you going to do that, Duch?' asked Gary.

'I've got a friend.'

Actually, it was two brilliant guys who were at Air Studios in Catford, South London. Sadly, the place has gone now but these guys could produce an incredible sound and, as they owed me a favour, they let us have a bit of studio time to make some demo tapes.

Getting the Artist and Repertoire guy at Island Records even to listen to the demos was a feat in itself, but we managed it. He was a young kid and thought the songs were excellent, but he wanted to send the demos off to a voice analyst.

This completely puzzled us. Why on earth would he want to do that?

It turned out that the guys at Island thought there were five people singing on the tapes, even though I had explained that it was just me.

'We wanted to be sure,' said the A&R guy when the tapes came back from the analyst.

'If all of the band could sing, then we might have signed you, even though you are a bit old for us,' he added. 'Boy bands look like they could be the thing of the future. Although I think the songs are good, we are not really signing up groups with lead singers at the moment. And the days of the singer/songwriters are well and truly over. But I'll tell you what I'll do ... Show us some more of your songs, Duch, and, if they are up to this quality, we might be able to do a deal for the publishing rights and maybe, only maybe, swing signing you as a solo artist. How about that?'

We also took the tapes to EMI who, once again, loved the songs and the production but again said they wanted a younger, five-boy singing group which they could mould and groom. It was only a year or so later that the most moulded and groomed boy band of all time, Take That, were launched.

Our lack of success in getting a recording deal led to the other guys deciding to leave and pursue their real careers in banks and on the trains.

But I held true to my dream and resumed playing in local pubs, busking and selling gear here and there to raise a little extra money.

The most important thing at the time was to get my songs heard and, with the rest of the guys in Harlequin having jobs and no time to perform, I knew I'd have to start from scratch again.

This time I decided to subscribe to a magazine which cost £60 a year but listed all the venues where they were looking for singers. It was run by an American guy named Eugene Jones. The first thing he had on offer for me was a talent night upstairs at the legendary Ronnie Scott's jazz club in Soho. Obviously, I jumped at the chance.

Michelle and a crowd of friends decided to come along and support me and they got down to the club in Frith Street about half-an-hour before I arrived.

When I got there, I had hassle straight away. As I walked up to the door on my crutches, this big bouncer said, 'And where do you think you're going, mate?'

'Inside,' I said. 'I'm singing here tonight.'

'No you ain't, mate, get lost.'

'But I'm booked to appear here,' I said, trying to sound a bit grand.

'Look,' the bouncer said, pointing at a poster. 'It says Nina Simone. Now unless my eyes are deceiving me, you ain't no Nina Simone. So hop it.'

'No, you don't understand ...'

'No, mate, it's you that don't understand ...'

Just at that moment, this young, fast-talking American guy came out of the club door and looked around.

'Don't tell me, you're Duchy Peter,' he said, holding out his hand. 'Eugene Jones.'

'Yeah, but ...'

'What on earth are you doing standing out here? Come on, this way. It's almost about to start.' And with that he yanked me into Ronnie Scott's. I looked at the bouncer and mouthed, 'Told ya,' as Eugene dragged me up the stairs.

There were about 12 people in the talent contest that night but I decided not to worry about them and just to concentrate on the three songs I'd chosen to perform. There was the inevitable 'I Can Hear the Children Crying', and another two – 'Long Love Water' and '4 Leaf'. I gave it my best shot, blotted out the audience and everyone else and went for it.

The evening dragged on and on as everyone got up to perform and, by the end, I had no idea if I had been any good or not.

But then the final judging was made and 'Ladies and gentlemen, tonight's winner of the Upstairs at Ronnie Scott's talent night is ... Duchy Peter.'

All my friends went crazy. Michelle came up and threw her arms around me and Eugene was pumping my arm shouting, 'Congratulations, champ,' in only the way Americans can.

My reward for that night was £30, which I could easily have earned in a couple of hours busking. But I said nothing.

'And that's not all,' enthused Eugene. 'You also get to play again next week! And this time it's at the Hard Rock Café. Whaddya think about that, Duchy?'

I mumbled some sort of appreciation.

The Hard Rock Café in Piccadilly was brilliant. There was the usual queue outside to get in but inside there was a smattering of celebrities. I noticed the actress Felicity Kendal was there and one of the stars of *Desmonds*, the TV sitcom about a black barber.

I was so desperate for some of that stardom to rub off on me that I gave another self-assured performance without feeling nervous at all.

Next up, I found myself playing at the Rock Garden in the Piazza at Covent Garden. And then I was booked for a spot at Brown's nightclub again in Covent Garden. At the time, Brown's was the top nightclub in the capital with its heavy door policy and special VIP room. Most of the stars who visited the club were so blasé that they never bothered to listen to who was playing. But I didn't care. This was one of the inner sanctums of the music business and I had managed to get a foot in the door.

I wasn't the only person performing there that night. There was a black guy who sang 'Baby, Please Don't Go' and he sang it so well I actually felt a bit shitty going on after him. Up 'til now, competition had never really bothered me because I have always had great faith in my own talent. But Brown's was a different league.

I went on and sang and thankfully I got plenty of applause. Then I got down off the stage and went to the bar for a drink.

I was aware of this black bird who was looking at me

but I didn't turn around or acknowledge her. I played it cool, as if I was used to being in Brown's and never let anything faze me. I paid for my drink and moved away from the bar.

A few weeks later, I bumped into my friend Marcia.

'What have you got against Mica these days, Duchy?'

'Nothing,' I said, genuinely bemused. Mica Paris had hit the big time with her debut album *So Good* and I think the brilliant 'Contribution' set had been released or was about to be released. 'I'm happy for her. I always said she'd make it. Fantastic voice.'

'Then how come you managed to snub her when you appeared at Brown's?'

'Did I?' I said. 'I don't remember even seeing her there.'

'Well, she saw you. Says you were right near her by the bar and then you just walked off.'

Oh no, I thought. And sadly, to this day, I haven't seen or spoken to Mica.

Although my musical career wasn't actually heading for the stratosphere, I believed I was moving in the right circles and I went back into the studio with the band at Thomas Dolby's old studios in Hammersmith. It was the best stuff I had done to date and I was pleased with it. Things seemed to be going OK.

Then, one day, I was down in Peckham, South London, when this elderly black guy with a trilby just stopped me in the street.

'How are you, Raymond?' he said.

'I'm sorry,' I said, 'I don't think I know you.'

'No, you wouldn't. But I know all about you. I'm a sort of friend of your father's. Me and your dad used to go drinking together before he became a Christian and gave up all that sort of thing.'

'That's interesting. I've never thought about him having a life before the church.'

'Oh yes. He was quite a man was your dad. He loved to have a drink and he loved the ladies. If you see him, give him my regards. Tell him George asked after him.'

'I'll do that,' I said.

'Oh, here's my bus now,' added George. 'Must be going. By the way, did Jeff tell you why he had both of you put into care? I could never figure that out, him being a Christian and everything.'

But, before I could reply, George had got on his bus. He smiled back at me as I was mouthing the words, 'Whaddya mean, *both* of us?'

The bus pulled away. Whether George heard me or not I'll never know, but he made no reply.

Both of us, I thought, *both* of us!

11

Paying the Rent

THE BELIEF THAT one day I'd make it as a musician, and Harlequin would appear at Wembley Arena, kept my dream alive for a few months as I slogged from pub to club. Then slowly, one by one, the club gigs started drying up and I didn't fancy going back to busking. The harsh truth was that I had to earn money to keep myself going and the only way I knew how to do it was through villainy, skulduggery and fear. If anyone had to have the frighteners put on them, call for Duchy. I was a black belt in martial arts and, even though I'd moved to Mottingham, I was still a Regulator. If there were any problems, people would say, 'Go and see Duchy, he'll sort it out with his fists, his crutches or his *nunchukas* – but he'll make sure it gets sorted.'

Respect is a wonderful thing to have, but it don't pay the rent. Selling gear does.

I'd hooked up with a cab driver named Gary who would

wheel me around when I was making my drops. I never had to explain to him why I was stopping here, there and everywhere – he just knew. There was something secretive and furtive about Gary. His eyes were dark, misty and shadowy. They were the eyes of someone who looked like he may have killed somebody. But nothing was ever said.

Then, one day, Gary asked me, 'What do you do weekends?'

'Not a lot. Play a bit of music with the guys, have a smoke … this and that.'

'Fancy doing some shooting?'

I looked at him thinking, I might be a Regulator, but I don't go around blowing people away.

As if he could read my mind, Gary said, 'I mean clay pigeon shooting, Duchy, clay pigeon shooting, mate.'

And that's how I ended up going down to Crockenhill near Swanley, known as the gateway to Kent, because it's countryside but still quite close to the centre of London.

We found this bit of disused marsh land which couldn't be developed but, if we gave this local geezer £5 a month, he'd let us up there to go shooting. Of course, there weren't any clay pigeons at all and I wasn't stupid enough to ask Gary where they were. It was all a bit of a gangster set-up.

'There's a few real pigeons around, and there are plenty of old pheasant if you want to try those,' said Gary. 'But we prefer to shoot trees.'

And then I realised exactly what this place was. It was where the criminal fraternity would meet to test out the latest guns. And there is no better way to test a gun than firing it at a tree. Trees are tough and they are hard, and most of them round Crockenhill were riddled with bullet holes.

I'd been involved in the gun trade back in East London but that was small-time compared with what was going on in Crockenhill.

One Sunday morning we were down there – me, Gary and about seven other mean-looking blokes. They all set up their guns, loading them and blasting away. Gary at the time had this savage pump-action shotgun which had a nozzle at the front. The nozzle would close the spray in and out. I was fascinated by this pump-action gun.

'Do you want a go?' Gary said to me.

'Not half.'

So he loaded it up and I remember my ears ringing for ages after the first shot. Gary used to pretend he was a bit of a gamekeeper, except he used a pump-action for bagging the birds and was never that good anyway. He'd point at a couple of pheasant way down in the next field, and – bang, bang. But the pheasants would just move, which was the signal for Gary to get closer – bang, bang.

Every weekend, Gary would bring me a new gun to try and he had some of the craziest weapons I've ever seen. One of them was called a Magnum Slugster. It was a new shotgun similar to the ones the police in America used at the time. They used to keep them across the top of the dashboard of their cars. It was a cool weapon. It came in a box about 3ft long by a foot wide.

'Have a look at this one, Duch,' said Gary. 'It's a beauty.'

And it was. I opened the box and the gun was broken into the butt, the barrel and the trigger mechanism. I soon got it out of the box and fitted the pieces together.

'Feel the weight,' said Gary. 'Feel the balance. I told you it was a beauty. Try it out, keep it for a while. I want 300 quid for it. It's a beauty.'

So the next morning, I went down to Crockenhill on my own with the Slugster. There was a road that ran into this land. On one side there were some travellers' sites and it was wide open on the other. I opened the gate quietly, because people lived there, drove my car in and closed the gate so the horses wouldn't get out, and then drove up this long winding country road. As I got halfway up the road, a pheasant ran across in front of the car.

I stopped the car, opened the box, screwed the Slugster together and carefully stalked the pheasant. It was a huge, old, ungainly bird and I'd soon got it in my sights. Bang. I saw a flutter, so I walked even nearer and gave it another one. Blow me if it wasn't the bird Gary had been trying to kill a few days earlier. That was the first – and last – pheasant I ever shot.

'So whaddya think?' said Gary the next time I saw him. 'It's a ...'

'Don't say it, Gary. I know what you mean. It's a beauty. And I'll tell you what,' I added, laughing, 'it's a lot better for shooting old pheasant than that pump-action you use. You'd better stick to trees, mate.'

Gary had a friend in Germany who would bring the guns over to the UK. There were handguns, shotguns, Dirty Harry-type Magnums, all different sorts, even little .22s. I'd test them for accuracy and penetration and, quietly, I'd start to punt out the guns to people who said they needed them. No questions asked.

'You ought to get one just for yourself, Duch,' said Gary one day. 'A bit of personal insurance so to speak.'

'Nah, I don't need one. I'm a martial artist, I don't need a gun. And, if ever I do, I know where I can get my hands on one. So I don't really need to carry one myself.'

'You never know.'

'Yeah, I do. People pack knives or guns because they are scared, whereas a real hard bastard can look after himself. And that's what I can do. I don't mind selling guns, but they are not really for me.'

By this time, I had set up a new fraternity in Mottingham. Little Marc and myself had decided to grow cannabis hydroponically at my house at the time, until we could get sorted out. Baz would run about, getting things for me that we needed. He was always going on about the skunk plans and I would say to him, 'Don't tell anyone, not anyone!'. Everyone was doing it. Home-grown skunk was the big thing, it was stronger and the profit margin was greater. But, growing drugs is a long and hard process and it was easier to sell a few guns.

I was doing about two or three pieces a week; some were to people I knew, some were Gary's friends and some were complete strangers. Some people would just want to rent a gun and bring it back the next day. But if the guy didn't bring it back, he knew we'd find him and someone would kill him. There was no doubt about that; no one was allowed to fuck with my guns.

But I had to be on my guard. In the old days, if a villain got into trouble with one of my guns, I probably wouldn't know about it for two or three years, that's how professional they were. Now any two-bit kid would want to get a gun to shoot someone over something fucking stupid like a parking space. Fortunately, idiots like that were easy to spot, and I'd make sure they never got their hands on a piece, at least not one of mine anyway.

Baz was a good man and a key member of our skunk operation. He was a short, stocky bloke but he knew his drugs. I was a bit surprised when, one day, he said, 'Duch, we've got to get into Charlie, coke, it's the new buzz, everyone's buying it.'

'Forget it,' I replied. 'We don't want anything to do with that shit. And you steer clear.'

But, of course, he couldn't. If it had been the odd line at

a party, maybe it would have been all right. But Baz had to go the whole hog.

I'd go down to his house in the mornings, and he was never out of bed. When he eventually roused himself, he would be puking his guts up, and there'd be blood and shit everywhere. I was quite worried about the boy. And it came to a head when I realised Baz had washed up the Charlie so he had more of it, and had run through £1,200 worth of our money in one go.

'You're not looking too well, Baz,' I'd say to him.

'Don't worry, Duch, I'm all right.'

But he wasn't. Baz wouldn't take no for an answer and his drug-taking soon started to affect the skunk operation. The whole operation was eventually brought down because of Baz's mad drug ways and outbursts. I was always picking up his shit and I was fucked off with it. One night, we went down to a club where the bouncers were my friends and they let me sell a bit of gear in there. It was £25 for the ordinary punter to get into the place but they used to charge Baz £5 because he was with me. But this night, Baz went into one and started shouting at the bouncers, 'How much ... how fucking much?'

'Five pounds, mate ... you got a problem with that?' said one of the bouncers who was about 6ft 6in tall and weighed in at around 20st. No one in their right mind would argue with someone like that. But Baz wasn't in his right mind.

'I don't see why I should have to pay,' he mouthed back. 'I'm here with Duchy.'

Obviously, he wasn't going to be let in and so I walked away and left him. But I was angry. I was angry because Baz had showed me up in front of my friends and that's a dreadful thing to do. I'd seen just how people like Baz can flip when they do cocaine and completely change. I realised now that we had a potential problem on our hands.

The next day, I took Baz to task about it.

'How dare you fucking well show me up in front of my mates,' I said to him. 'Me and those guys go back years and you're endangering everything because of your cocky attitude and addiction to crack. Don't deny it, Baz, I've seen the way you are and I've seen the amount of money you're getting through, wads of it. Now either you clean yourself up or you're out.'

There was a silence and then Baz put his head in his hands and said quietly, 'You don't know what I'm going through.'

'Then tell me.'

I knew that Baz's dad had been wealthy and had recently died but I didn't know that he had left Baz a string of kebab shops. Under the terms of the Will, they were being run by Baz's relative, and the profits should have been going into Baz's bank account.

But it seems that everyone wanted a piece of the action. One night, his mum's car got burned out and then some guys threatened Baz himself. And these incidents were going on one after another.

I had an idea who might be behind it – the Arif family – who were a notorious Turkish firm, but I couldn't prove anything, it was just a hunch. The rest of the guys in my fraternity wanted to go down and smash up the Arifs and teach them a lesson because Baz was one of ours. But I told them to slow down and show a bit of restraint.

'One, we don't know for sure it is the Arifs and, two, we don't know a lot about their firm,' I told them. 'Turkish firms are like Chinese ones, they keep themselves to themselves.'

If it had been the Arifs, I knew I could sort it out as I knew one of them. So after a little digging around, it turned out that

Baz's family had nothing to do with the Arifs. That meant this little firm was bang in trouble.

Baz was also convinced that his relative was robbing him blind, and other members of his family had arranged for a woman to come over from Turkey to contest the Will and cut this relative out of it all together. But, when he got a whiff of what was going on, there was an almighty row. Baz's relative went round to Baz's house where Baz pulled a knife on him and was promptly thrown down the stairs.

As soon as I heard of the latest incident, I knew that measures had to be taken.

'Get your relative to come along to a meeting. And I'll be there, too,' I told Baz. 'This has got to be sorted one way or another. It's not only affecting you and your bloody crack habit but it's spilling over into our firm. It's got to be sorted now.'

So Baz arranged the meeting and this Turkish geezer showed up. He was in his late thirties/early forties, and well dressed with a gun under his t-shirt. He's old enough to know better, I thought as I sized him up.

All of a sudden, he started gabbing away in Turkish and I didn't understand a word he said.

'What's he on about, Baz?' I asked.

'Nothing.'

'It must be bloody something.'

Then I heard a few words in English, 'You have to do this … you must get rid of her.'

'What's he asking you to do, Baz?'

'Nothing.'

Because I had interrupted things, his relative suddenly demanded to know who I was.

'He's my friend,' said Baz.

'Why's he here?'

At that I just switched; I think I went a bit nuts. I said, 'Mate, you're treating this bloke like shit. You're supposed to be his family. You're meant to be looking after him and putting money in his bank account, and you're not. You're robbing him. You're scum ... do you understand what I'm sayin'?'

'Perfectly,' he replied quite calmly and then glanced down at the waistband of his trousers. It was only a split-second glance, but it was long enough for me to understand he was checking himself out to make sure he was carrying a shooter.

Alarm bells were ringing in my head and I could hear what Gary had forever been telling me, 'You ought to get one for yourself, Duch. A bit of personal insurance so to speak.'

Well, it was too late now. And what I really thought was, Cheeky bastard, fancy coming to a meeting with your nephew and turning up with a shooter.

I decided it was best to take the initiative and looked the relative straight in the eyes. I whispered to him, 'How can you come and see one of your own family while you're packing?'

He blinked, and at that point I leaped across the table and went for the waistband of his trousers in an attempt to grab the gun.

He went for the gun, too, and we both wrestled for it. I just managed to get there first and I could feel my finger on the trigger. He was starting to sweat.

'I was right then, wasn't I?' I said as calmly as possible. 'Now, what if I shoot you, you cunt ... what if I shoot you? Any reason why I shouldn't?'

In fact, I knew a damn good reason why I shouldn't. There was a hairdresser's downstairs and they would have heard the bang.

He then grabbed my arm in a vice-like grip and my finger

205

slipped off the trigger while I tried to pull the gun out of the waistband.

'Let go,' I shouted, and moved my other arm down to the pocket of my trousers. 'Let go or I'll take out my gun and I'll shoot you stone dead right here.'

It was a stand-off; he didn't know if I was bluffing or not but he wouldn't take the chance.

He took his grip off my arm, and calmly opened up a packet of fags and lit one up. I slowly pulled my hand away from the waistband of his trousers.

'That's better,' I said. 'Let's all take it nice and easy, after all, this is family.'

After a silent pause, Baz's relative said to me, 'I don't even know your name.'

'Duchy,' I replied. 'Just call me Duchy.'

'Well, you must be a good friend of Baz's.'

'Yes I am, we're practically brothers. He works for a little firm of mine, and we stick together.'

Then the relative started going on about how his brother was such a good man and one thing and another, and then right out of the blue he started crying.

I nearly shit myself. I thought, Watch it, he's unstable and he's still got a gun.

After he managed to pull himself together, he looked at me and said, 'Why don't you show me your gun, Duchy?'

'Why don't you show me yours?'

And he pulled out a little .22 from the waistband.

'Now you.'

'I don't show my gun to anyone,' I replied.

'Yeah, well, I'm special.'

'Whaddya mean special?'

'A special, a special constable.' And he flicked open a piece of paper or a badge or something.

I thought, Fucking hell, this is getting weirder. So I put my hands up and, with a laugh, I said, 'What gun? Look, I ain't got no gun. I don't carry guns. Why should I risk getting in my car with my gun to drive down here to humiliate you when I could easily pick up a phone afterwards and have you nicely tucked away?' And I gave him a big smile.

And right at that second, I picked up one of my crutches and knocked away his gun from the table.

As it went skidding over the floor, he instinctively bent down to try and pick it up. With that, I brought the crutch down full-force on his neck, shouting, 'Special constables aren't supposed to carry guns, do you understand that? Am I making myself clear? Pick him up, Baz.'

Baz did as he was told and sat his relative back in the chair.

'Now I don't know what you think your game is, mate, but it's over.'

His game, in fact, had been a big one. He had brought the gun to give to Baz who was really a bit of a stupid young kid. And he wanted Baz to shoot the woman who had come over from Turkey to contest the Will. That's why he kept saying, 'You must do something about this woman, she is a problem to us. You must be a man and do the manly thing. You know what I want you to do, don't you?'

If his relative had managed to get the woman killed and Baz nicked for it, then he would have had all those kebab shops to himself. Over my dead body, he would.

Baz never had any more trouble from him after I'd taught him a lesson, and he even managed to clean up his cocaine habit, which I thought was a right result.

While I was trying to keep my firm together in Mottingham, I also had new friends down in Swanley near the Crockenhill firing range. One of them was this very well-dressed guy named Doug who had a large house and drove a very nice car.

He was a black guy and used to hang around with a white guy called Reg and they both soon got nicknamed Crockett and Tubbs from the old *Miami Vice* TV show.

They both seemed pretty genuine and Doug even remortgaged his house so they could buy sacks of grass and hash and really get into the dealing business.

I'd spent quite a lot of time with these two, training with them in the morning and getting to know them. But we didn't talk business, I was always told by top people never to get in the way of men's business.

I didn't think that they would become a problem until Little Mark and Jimmy noticed they were moving about our manor with a lot of gear and Charlie.

Jimmy said to me one day, 'You know Crockett and Tubbs?'

'Yeah.'

'Well, I think they are trying to take over the manor.'

'Whaddya mean?'

'They are muscling in on our business,' added Jimmy. 'And from what I can see, it's the white bloke that's making all the running.'

'His name's Reg.'

'Yeah, I know, and I'm keeping an eye on him.'

Jimmy was right, things were going pear-shaped for our firm and we were only managing to sell a small quantity of gear, hardly enough to keep ourselves fed. I was really skint at the time and challenged Doug over it, which resulted in a threatening row and left us no longer on speaking terms.

Doug was the man who provided all the money in his little set-up with Reg, and Reg did all the leg work.

Little Mark came up to me and said, 'Duch, you know that guy that's running around with Doug, well, he's a robber. He asked me to sell him a kilo for 1,800 quid and then tell Doug it was 2,400 while he pocketed the money for himself.'

'I couldn't bloody well care,' I replied. 'I'm not speaking to Doug meself, so, if he's being stupid, that's up to him.'

This all happened around one Christmas time. It should have been a good time for me, but no. There were only a few club gigs to play and little or no gear to sell. In fact, it was one of the most miserable Christmases I can remember. Michelle had left and, although there was no animosity between us and I could see the kids whenever I liked, it was still a lonely time for me.

In the first week of the New Year, there was a knock on my door and who should be standing there but Doug. I was shocked to see him because we hadn't spoken over Christmas and I was still fuming about having no money.

He wanted to know if I fancied going round his house. I knew it must have taken him a lot of bottle to break the ice and so I put my coat on and went with him.

Once in his car, he started telling me a story about a friend of his who got into business with another guy and then found out he was losing money. This was going missing, that was going missing, money wasn't adding up.

'Stop right there, Doug,' I said. 'I'm going to have a wild guess now, but you wouldn't be talking about you and Reg, would you?'

'Well, yes, Duchy, I am, I'm ashamed to say.'

'Doug, I've known Reg has been bleeding you for ages. But, as we were no longer mates, I didn't think it was important.'

'Well, it is important and I want your help.'

Then it all came tumbling out. How Reg had been ripping

Doug off for thousands of pounds. And how it was Reg who had been trying to kill off my business and bad-rapping me behind my back.

'Well, I think we need to teach him a lesson,' I said to Doug.

We arranged to meet Reg at around 7.00pm that night. We drove down to Catford in South London after Doug had contacted Reg to tell him that he had the gear and would be bringing it along. And if four big geezers turn up in a white van, then you know you are going somewhere.

Reg jumped into the van and said, 'How are you, Doug … have you got the stuff?'

But, before Doug could reply, I tapped Reg on the shoulder and said, 'How dare you say to Doug that I'm a waste of space.'

He turned around and he was looking down the barrel of a gun.

'Hello, Duch,' he managed to stammer. 'What kind of game's this?'

'It ain't no game, Reg.'

We kidnapped him and took him to Crockenhill.

'We know what you've been up to, Reg,' said Doug. 'And now Duchy's going to deal with you. Ain't that right, Duch?'

'It certainly is.'

Reg started crying and saying that he didn't mean it and that he'd pay back the money.

'Quit bawling,' I shouted. 'Or I'll do you here.' And I thrust the barrel of the gun straight into his face.

Doug interrupted, 'No one will hear from you any more. You've been robbing me blind and you got me to blow my man Duchy out so you could fleece me. Say goodbye, Reg.'

At this, Reg started crying even more. Apparently, he had stolen more than £12,000 off Doug. Their wives used to go out together and Doug's wife always wondered why Reg's had plenty of money and she hadn't, even though they were in the same business together. Reg would gamble the money and then phone Doug from casinos to gloat.

When we got to Crockenhill, Reg was thrown roughly out of the van and I thrust a shovel into his hand.

'Dig,' I commanded.

While he started digging, we were hurling abuse at him and tears were rolling down his cheeks.

'Dig faster,' I'd shout.

'I've had enough of this,' said Doug. 'Let's shoot him now.'

'Please, please don't,' Reg was screaming. 'I'll do anything, anything at all.'

'The only thing you're going to do is hurry up and finish your grave,' I said.

While he was doing that, I took his mobile phone. 'Look, Doug,' I said nonchalantly. 'He's got all the numbers in here of his mates. Let's get him to phone them all up and tell them that he's got this amazing gear for them.'

'I'll do it, I'll do it,' begged Reg. 'Please, please don't shoot me.'

So he started making these phone calls, but I could see he was playing for time. He kept saying, 'There's no one there.'

'Well, there had better be,' I said.

After about 30 minutes, I turned to Doug and said, 'You're right, this is stupid, Doug. Let's shoot him now.'

And, as if by a miracle, some of the numbers were answered.

He eventually got through to about ten of his friends and told them to bring their money and come for the gear. We stuck Reg back in the van and drove all over London meeting his mates. Reg managed to talk them into handing over the cash and said he would have the gear for them later that night. By the end of the evening, we had made about £14,000, which paid off his debt to Doug. Of course, no gear was ever delivered and Reg's former colleagues and mates are probably still baying for his blood.

We took him back to my place in Mottingham where we handcuffed him to a radiator. 'This is for your own good, Reg,' I explained. 'If that mob you've just ripped off get their hands on you, they'll tear you to pieces'.

'Don't kill me, Duch, please don't kill me.'

Doug interrupted, 'He ain't gonna kill you, Reg. We are going to let you go when all this is over.'

You could see the relief pour over Reg's face.

'I'm sorry, Doug,' I said, 'but I am … I'm gonna kill him as soon as this is over.'

Then we bundled him back in the van, stripped him to his underwear and took him up to the M25. And that's where we let him go. And we've never heard from him since.

Although we had got a result and no one was hurt, except for Reg's mates who lost their money, I couldn't help feeling that I was letting myself down. My dream had been to play my music, not run around threatening people with guns.

We'd even got kind of a manager who promised me and Harlequin just about everything. He got us studio time and told us how much he believed in the music. The other lads in the band were about to give up their day jobs because they were so impressed by him. Unfortunately, he left us several hundred quid in debt for the studio time and no way could we afford to pay it. It was just another big headache to try and live with.

We sent a tape of the studio work we had done to EMI Records and they were very interested; the feedback from the company was really positive. But EMI got in touch with our 'manager' and he managed to fuck it up again for us. He kept going on to them about disabilities as if it was some sort of gimmick. Just because a bloke's on crutches doesn't mean he can't sing as well as anyone else, and he should be treated the same.

EMI got a bit cagey about Harlequin because they didn't think they could market a disabled singer and so we got knocked back on that. It really disheartened the guys in the band but I just thought, So what? I've never had a decent break anyway. And I just carried on as usual.

About that time, Jimmy came up to me and said, 'Duchy, I hear some blokes have been up to your parents' house hassling them. I don't know what it's about but the word is it's those geezers that hang out in the snooker hall, the Rastafarian guys.'

I went fucking mad. 'Cheers, Jimmy,' I said. But I was fuming. I might not have got on very well with my parents over the years, but nobody was going to mess with them.

I got hold of a gun, and went straight down to the snooker hall. I wasn't even thinking what I was doing. It was only when I got there that I realised I could easily be killed because these were bad boys, very bad boys. They were all black Yardies and they usually all packed guns.

When I got there, they were sitting around playing dominoes.

I stared straight at them. 'Which one of you lot went to my mum and dad's house?' I said.

No one answered and I wasn't surprised. I didn't think any of them would declare themselves. I turned to one guy who looked a bit more sure of himself. If I was going to shoot anyone, it would have been him.

I pointed at him, 'Do you know who went up to Forest Hill? Somebody knows.'

If the guy had kept his head down, he would have been all right, but he was looking at me with attitude, he had a sneer on his face as if to say, 'I'm not scared of you.'

'All lost our tongues, have we?' I added. 'Well, wait there, I'm coming back.'

With that, I went to my car and got my gun, loaded it and walked back towards the snooker hall.

As I approached, I heard a shout behind me: 'Duchy, Duchy ... Duchy.' It was a mate of my cousin's who'd begged me not to go back in the hall and shoot those boys. 'Don't do it, Duchy,' he pleaded.

'Fuck 'em,' I said. 'They shouldn't mess with my mum and dad.' And I continued towards the snooker hall.

But, when I got there, I saw the last of them leaving by the back door. The Yardies had been shit scared. But something niggled me about it all. When you have a gun in your hand, people do whatever you want. If I'd punched the lights out of those guys before I got any respect, I would have had to take on lots of them. But threaten them with a gun and they sit up and listen.

It has its value – but it wasn't my way. Instead of being a hard bastard and a Regulator, I was turning into nothing more than a punk with a shooter in my hand.

I'd approached the problem the wrong way from the beginning. First, I should have gone to see my mum and dad and found out exactly what had been going on. And that's what I decided to do. There were a few answers I wanted from them anyway and they had been long overdue. It was time to clear the air completely.

Mum answered the door looking neat and tidy as usual and with an expression of surprise on her face.

'Oh, son, this is a pleasure,' she said. 'Come in.'

We had a cup of tea and chatted a bit, then I said, 'Mum,

did some black guys come round here and disturb you?'

'Yes they did, Duch. I didn't think to bother to tell you. I didn't want you to get into trouble.'

'What was it all about?'

'Something about a dog – one of those Dobermans you breed, I think. This one gentleman was angry, kept claiming it wasn't a real Doberman but a cross.'

'Was that it?' I said, amazed. 'Something as piddling as that.'

'Please, Raymond, mind your language. Anyway, your dad sent them packing.'

'He did what?'

'He sent them packing with a flea in their ear and told them you would deal with them when you caught them up.'

I was amazed; here was my father taking my side.

'Oh, and he likes that music tape you sent him. He thinks you've got a good voice and good songs. And he sent a cheque to the studio to pay for the recording time.'

'He did what?'

'Don't keep repeating yourself, Raymond. Anyway, your dad's only just popped out. He'll be back in a minute if you're stopping. Want another cup of tea?'

'Yes, I'd love one. And I will stay because there are a few questions I want to ask you and Dad.'

'Like what, son?'

'Well, for a start, Mum … am I a twin?'

12

Family Fortunes

'WHAT ON EARTH makes you think that, son?' she asked, quite taken aback. 'No, of course you're not a twin. There's only one Duch Peter in the world.' And she tried to laugh, but it was a false laugh as if she knew that I was probing into secrets that had lain dormant for years. But she also gave a barely audible sigh and I realised that the truth was about to come tumbling out.

'I bumped into an old friend of Dad's,' I said.

'Oh yes, where was that?'

'Down in Peckham. His name was George, said he used to work with Dad before he became a Reverend.'

I could see Mum slightly stiffen. 'George … George … I don't remember any George,' she said.

'Well, it was a long time ago, Mum. But it was more what he said.'

'What was he doing, filling your head with nonsense?'

'No, no, I don't think he was. In fact, he was putting me straight. He said he couldn't figure out why Dad, being a Christian, put *both* of us into care. Mum, what did he mean by "both of us"?'

There was silence.

'Sit down, son. I suppose you will have to know. And I don't want you to blame your dad. Things happened a long time ago.'

'What kind of things?'

'Well … the fact is, Raymond …' She hesitated. 'You have an elder sister. There. Now I've said it.'

'A sister!' I echoed incredulously.

'Yes, her name is Sheila.'

'Sheila! But where is she? Why didn't anyone tell me this before?'

'It was your father's decision to keep things quiet at the beginning and then over the years … well, you know how things are, some things are better left unsaid.'

'But where is she now, Mum?'

'She lives in Catford, in a home.'

'A home?'

'Yes, Raymond, you see she was born mentally handicapped and, at the time, it was decided …'

'To lock her away, just like you tried to lock me away,' I shouted as I jumped up, anger in my face.

'No, no, it wasn't like that at all, believe me. She was severely handicapped and I just couldn't cope with the responsibility and everything else. Your dad thought it was best if professionals looked after her.'

I sat down again and tried to stay calm as Mum, with tears in her eyes, told me the truth that had been hidden from me for so many years.

Sheila was five years older than me and there were

complications with her birth. The head wasn't in the correct position and it was decided that forceps would have to be used to assist in pulling the baby out. But something went wrong and a side of her brain was damaged during the delivery causing her to be mentally handicapped.

Mum started crying as she relived the trauma. And then she added quietly, 'I still go and see her. I still go and visit her in the home, son. I've always loved her.'

I put my arm around her. 'I'm sure you have, Mum, I'm sure you have,' I said.

The silence was broken by a key turning in the front-door lock. 'That'll be your dad,' she said, wiping away tears with her apron and starting to get agitated.

'Now don't worry yourself, Mum. I'll handle this. Go and make us a nice cup of tea.'

What exactly I was going to handle, I had no idea. But there was a rising tide of anger inside me. Dad stepped into the sitting room and took in the whole scene in a second.

'Hello, Raymond … what are you doing here? In more trouble, are you?'

'No, I'm not, Dad. First, I came round here to thank you for paying off the studio bill we ran up when that so-called manager left us in the lurch.'

For an instant, I actually thought he looked embarrassed.

'And I've been having a bit of a chat with Mum.'

At that moment, Mum burst into the room from the kitchen and blurted out, 'I've told him, Jeff, I've told him all about Sheila. I had to. An old friend of yours, George somebody, mentioned it to him and he had practically guessed the truth.'

My father's face was totally expressionless as he calmly said, 'Oh, I see, so now you know about Sheila, do you? Now you know about Sheila Baker.'

I looked puzzled. 'Baker?' I said. 'But our name is Peter. Isn't Baker Mum's maiden name?'

'You heard what I said, Raymond,' Dad replied.

And then the penny dropped: someone else had fathered Sheila. My eyes narrowed as I stared at him. I thought to myself, I don't care what reasons he uses to excuse himself for putting me and my sister in a home. But I blurted out, 'Why did you give me away to foster parents? Why did you make me endure years in children's homes?'

'You know why, Raymond. You were a thalidomide baby. Your mother wasn't able to cope with you. After the trauma she had gone through with the birth of Sheila and then you coming along a few years later, it was too much for her to stand.'

I looked at Mum, who lowered her eyes to the carpet.

'But not all thalidomide babies were given away at birth,' I protested. 'Most families were loving and looked after their children.' I spat out the words as I looked Dad straight in the eye. He never even blinked.

'In your case, that was the decision that was made. Now let that be an end of it.'

'But there were grants you could get to look after disabled kids. And the company that made thalidomide was forced to pay compensation.'

'I said that's the end of it, Raymond. Now I'm going out again. I only came to get a set of keys. There's something that needs to be done at the church. You know about Sheila … surely that's enough for one day.'

As he went back into the hall, I wanted to shout at him, 'Always playing the man of the cloth, aren't you, Dad?' But the words wouldn't leave my mouth.

But it was as if he knew and he turned round and said, 'If you had paid more attention to the Lord, Raymond, maybe your life wouldn't have been one of constantly shuffling in and out of prison. You disappoint me.'

'And what do you think you do to me?'

'Raymond,' interrupted Mum. 'I won't have you talk to your father like that.'

'What father? He's never treated me like a real father would. I'm just an embarrassment to him.'

'Now stop it,' she added.

And, as the front door banged shut, I heard my father mutter, 'Past sins, past sins. This is the result.'

I turned to Mum. 'He's crazy. What did he mean by that?'

'He's not crazy. He just has very strong-held beliefs. Now sit down again and drink that tea I made for you.'

There were still so many unanswered questions and the only way to get all the answers was by staying calm and listening to Mum. After all, she had put up with Dad for years and knew exactly how his mind worked.

'What did he mean by past sins, Mum?' I asked.

She sighed again. 'Well, I can see you realised why your sister Sheila is a Baker and not a Peter, but that wasn't the kind of sins he was referring to. Jeff believes that we are all sinners in the eyes of God and that we are judged by him because of our past sins. It wasn't so much he thought we couldn't look after you when you were born, but that your disability was due to past sins, that in some way God was punishing him by having you born a thalidomide baby. And the fact that Sheila had also been born with a handicap only helped to confirm his ideas. You were the result of him being a sinner in the past.'

'But that's crazy.'

'Maybe to you, son, but not to your father.'

'And is that why he became a Reverend?'

'Well, he won't admit it, but, yes, I do think it was a way of him trying to atone for his sins.'

'And so he had me given away at birth? Was that another way of atoning?' I said sarcastically.

It passed without comment but I could see my mum looked weary and worn out and my heart went out to her. Not only had she had to put up with a God-fearing husband, but she had tried to do it all with a smile while hiding the secret of having a mentally handicapped daughter.

I put my hand on hers. 'You know, Mum,' I said, 'if it's all right by you, I wouldn't mind coming with you when you next go and visit our Sheila. After all, she is me sister.'

Her eyes brightened. 'Would you, Raymond, would you really?'

'Of course I would. I'd love to.'

Then she suddenly changed tack. 'You know what you said earlier, about compensation for being a thalidomide child?'

'Yeah.'

'Well, you might as well know the truth about that as well.'

'Go on.'

'We were offered compensation. But your dad turned it down.'

'He did what?'

'You heard. He turned it down. He turned it down because he believed that your handicap was the will of God and that God would provide. Now will you please just leave it at that.'

'But how much did he turn down, Mum?' I asked innocently.

There was a pause. 'Well, we were offered £63,000, but he wouldn't take a penny of it.'

'Sixty-three grand!' I exploded. '*Sixty-three grand!*'

Now I was convinced he was mad. And I was angry. I still

am. With that amount of money in those days, they could have got help to take care of me. It wouldn't have made up for my disability, but at least it would have helped soften the blow. I am still angry now about how it all turned out. I was seething when Mum first told me, but I couldn't take it out on her.

So I said quietly, 'Before I let things drop, just tell me one more thing.'

'What's that?'

'Just tell me why, if it had been decided to put me into foster homes as soon as I was born, did you come and find me again when I was with the Rodriguez family?'

'That was your dad. I think by then he realised what he had done and …'

I finished the sentence for her, 'Felt guilty?'

'Maybe, son, maybe.'

I put my arm round her. 'Never mind, Mum.' I said. 'Never mind. At least now I've got a sister.'

My head was reeling when I left the house in Forest Hill. Everything was fitting into place but it was an awful truth that I had to face. I had never particularly liked my dad because he was always religious and held so many bigoted points of view. But I found it unforgivable of him to give me away as a child because he believed I was a result of some past sin. It was idiotic, it was stupid. But, above all else, it was hardly Christian.

I could sympathise with my mother, though. I really don't think she could have coped with looking after Sheila, me and my father at the same time. She chose to stay with Dad, give me to the Cowards and declare my sister non-existent. But the funny thing is that I would never have known anything about it if George hadn't come up to me that day in Peckham. Maybe it was George's way of getting back at my father for some slight he might have suffered in the past. Whatever the reason, it had worked. And the Peter family would never be the same again.

OK, I had never been an angel by any stretch of the imagination. In and out of prison, fighting, stealing, selling drugs, selling guns. And I make no apologies for my lifestyle. I'm not going to blame the foster care, the children's homes or even my father. I am what I am. But not once, *not once*, did my dad put his arm around me and make me feel as if I belonged.

Every time I had tried to get on the good side of my old man, he'd say, 'You're a villain, you can't possibly know anyone nice. You shoot people, you stab people, you thieve. You're a den of iniquity.'

My dad hated me so much that, even if I bought my mum a present, he wouldn't let her have it, in case I had stolen it. We had never agreed on anything and we weren't similar in any way. He would wear a clean suit and I'd wear jeans, T-shirt and leather jacket – the dirtier the better. He believed in marriage and fidelity whereas I believed in bird after bird. He believed in owning your own house and that anyone living in a council flat was no better than rubbish. He believed in going to work; I believed in selling drugs. No wonder by the time I had grown up he had truly convinced himself that I was the result of past sins.

I remember when 'Chelle was pregnant with DJ and I told my mum. She made a bit of a hoo-ha about it and told me not to tell Dad because we weren't married and he didn't like to hear things like that. So I went straight up to him and said, 'Guess what, Dad? Michelle's expecting a baby and we have no intention of ever getting married. Just thought you might like to know.'

I would do anything to upset my old man just to make a point. And initially, after I found out the secret of Sheila and the ridiculous reason for giving me away at birth, I exploded with rage at my dad. Then, just as suddenly, I started to calm down and see things differently. I realised that not only was he a hypocrite and self-deluded, but he was also flawed; he was also human. And, instead of hating him any more, I pitied him.

Over the years, I had stopped being conscious about my disability and my artificial legs. On the streets of the East End, and south of the river, I had proved that I was equal to anyone. But the day I first went with Mum to visit Sheila in the home, I was all too conscious of it.

Clat … clat … clat … clat … As I walked across the lino floor of the reception area, the old, familiar sound reverberated around me. I kept thinking, I must try and be a little quieter, I'm drawing attention to myself. I must try and be a little quieter for Sheila's sake.

I had been looking forward to meeting my sister but it had been with some trepidation. I had grown up in institutions and I knew all about the bad things that went on inside. Anyone who tells you there aren't bad things going on inside some of those places is lying.

When I first met my sister, she was sitting in the day-room at the home. Her neck lolled forward as if she was asleep and she was dribbling from her mouth.

'Hello, Sheila,' said Mum sweetly. 'I've brought someone to see you.'

There was hardly a hint of recognition.

Mum continued, 'It's your brother, it's your brother, Raymond. You didn't know you had a brother Raymond, did you?'

Suddenly, I was more conscious than ever of my disability. Then Sheila looked up, her eyes completely vacant as Mum dabbed some spittle away from her chin.

225

'Gary-puh, gary-puh,' said Sheila, or something like that.

'What's she trying to say, Mum?' I asked.

'She's saying, "How are you?" Aren't you, darling?'

'Gary-puh.'

I put out my arms to hold her. 'I'm fine, sis,' I said, barely audible. 'I'm fine.' Tears started to well up in my eyes.

My sister really had no idea who I was at the time and I was so shocked by her appearance that I thought she was much worse than she really is.

Later, the more visits I made, the more I realised she was actually quite sensible. She couldn't make herself understood very easily, and she couldn't do a lot of things for herself but, in fact, her memory worked very well and never once has she forgotten to send me a birthday card or a Christmas present.

But, during the early visits, I used to harass the staff, accusing them of all sorts of things and calling them liars for telling me my sister was all right. I was obsessed by the fact – absolutely wrongly in fact – that she might have been abused in some way but no one was telling.

On the way home on the bus after the first visit, I was still shocked and unable to say very much. Mum tried to change the subject.

'Your dad's having sleepless nights,' she said.

'Good.'

Then she gave one of her sighs again and I realised she was getting weary of everything.

'I'm sorry, Mum,' I said. 'What's his problem?'

'It's the roof on the house. It's leaking and he's having nightmares about it.'

'Well, can't he get it fixed?'

'No he can't, Raymond,' she replied crossly. 'He's been quoted hundreds and hundreds of pounds just to put up the scaffolding to have a look at the problem and we can't even afford that, let alone getting it fixed. It's driving him crazy with worry.'

I didn't really give a fuck about my dad, but what he worried about my mum worried about.

At the time, I had a mate called Charlie Hooper whom I had met when he came up to me out of the blue and asked to buy some gear. I thought he was either stupid or had a death-wish to go up to a stranger and ask to buy drugs. I had never sold to anyone I didn't know, but I admired Charlie's bottle. And it turned out Charlie was a roofer.

Over a pint, I explained to Charlie about the leaking roof that my dad was obsessed with in Forest Hill.

'Them houses are 40ft high,' said Charlie. 'You'll need scaffolding to get up there and look at it.'

'I know that, Charlie, but he can't afford scaffolding. You got any ladders?'

'Well, yeah, but I ain't going up them.'

'In which case, I will bloody well go up them meself.'

And that's exactly what I attempted to do.

Dad was livid when I told him about my plan. 'I absolutely forbid it, Raymond,' he said. 'It's plain suicide, even for an able-bodied person. But for someone with your disability, well ... I'm speechless.'

'That'll be the first time,' I replied as I started my ascent up Charlie's rickety ladders. But, when Dad saw that there was no turning back, he gripped on to the bottom of the ladders to keep them still for me.

Halfway up, I nearly made a fatal error and started to look down. It was so frightening that I forced myself to concentrate on the climb and keep looking up towards the guttering and the roof.

Slowly, one artificial leg at a time, I hauled myself up the ladder until I finally got on to the roof.

I clambered all over it, inspecting every inch of the roof until I found the problem, which turned out to be a tear in one of the valleys. Absolutely sure there weren't any more problems, I inched my way down the ladder and back to safety.

As soon as I told Charlie the problem, he came up with a solution. We wouldn't have to put scaffolding all round the house, just up to the valley, which meant we could save hundreds of pounds in costs. Charlie carried out the job like the expert he is and that roof has never leaked again.

The effect it had on my father was miraculous. He was so shocked that I could contribute something to his life that he started treating me like a real son. I'd go round to his place and help with things round the house and, slowly, a real father and son relationship started to develop. It might have been 30 years too late, but it was better late than never.

Of course, he never approved of all the villainous things I got up to and, at the time, they were escalating out of control again. And he never approved of the clothes I wore. But he stopped criticising me for the sake of it. And, slowly, if he could find any redeeming feature in my lifestyle, then he would mention it.

He continued listening to the music I was making and, even if he didn't understand it that well, he would encourage me to keep at it.

'One day you'll make it as a musician and a singer, Raymond, I'm sure of it,' he would say. 'But you must persevere. You won't get anywhere without hard work.'

Equally slowly, I came to try and understand his values, although wearing a poxy suit is still never going to be for me.

* * *

Although I hadn't been to prison for years, I was still up to my old tricks and got most of my large quantities of gear, when I wasn't growing it myself, from a geezer named Dallas who was a real force to be reckoned with. He was the sort of bloke who demanded respect but, sadly, a few months after I got to know him, he died.

It was a major shock and he left a big legacy behind which no one could fill. Then, one day, I bumped into Dallas's wife, Nicole, and she asked me if I would run her husband's old fraternity, which I thought was crazy because Dallas knew some really serious people.

'Please, Duchy,' she said. 'Dallas trusted you. And I can't run it all on my own. I've tried, but it needs someone with your experience to keep it together.'

This meeting happened quite a few months after Dallas had died and, by then, Nicole had got a new boyfriend.

'What about that new bloke you're with?' I replied. 'Can't he help ya?'

'No, he can't, Duch. He hasn't got the experience. That's why I need you … now will you do it?'

Next thing I knew, I was cashing up in the evenings over in Dartford at Nicole's nice house and things were going smoothly again. I didn't pay much attention to the boyfriend at first until he started poking his nose in where it wasn't wanted. He was always in my face asking me about contacts and one thing and another. Of course, I kept stum.

'You can tell me, Duch,' he would say. 'I'm Nicole's boyfriend.'

'In which case, mate, if Nicole wants you to know anything she will tell you herself.'

He was becoming a pain in the arse, but it didn't bother me too much because he was a nobody. Then one day I got a phone call from Nicole telling me she had broken off her relationship with the bloke but he wouldn't take no for an answer. For a strong and usually calm woman, she was surprisingly agitated on the phone.

'What's he been up to?' I asked.

'Prowling round outside the house, hiding in the bushes. Duch, I think he's stalking me,' she replied, with a quiver in her voice. 'He's also been phoning and saying he wants money. I'm worried about the kids, Duchy.'

'Has he done anything else?'

'Well …' She paused.

'Well what?'

'He accused me of sleeping with a cripple black bastard.'

That did it.

Nicole gave me his phone number and I called him. I tried to be as calm and reasonable as possible. I told him that Nicole wanted nothing more to do with him and he should stop harassing her and the kids. I told him that he had become a problem and it was best for him if he took that problem elsewhere. 'And if I hear one more time that you've called me a cripple black bastard,' I said menacingly, 'then I'm gonna have to shoot ya.'

His laughter was still ringing in my ears when I jumped in the car. I drove straight round to my mate Eddie's, picked him up and a couple of guns, then drove down to Nicole's house. I bundled her in the car and the three of us high-tailed it to Maidstone where her ex-boyfriend lived.

I had hardly spoken I was so angry. But, when we were all in the car and approaching Maidstone, I turned to Nicole and said, 'OK, where does he live?'

'I don't know, Duch.'

'Whaddya mean you don't know?'

'Well, I don't know the exact address. I've only been there once. He was always more keen on coming to my place.'

'Oh, for Christ's sake.'

We were driving up and down streets and around roundabouts as Nicole tried to remember where he lived. It seemed a hopeless task because we didn't even know the correct name of the road we were looking for.

We were about to give it up as a bad job when Nicole's eyes lit up and she pointed out of the window shouting, 'There it is, there it is, that's his house.'

It was a large house with a drive, so Eddie and I got our guns, loaded them and walked towards the front door. The front of the house had this huge plate-glass window and I spotted him through it. He was reading a newspaper. Unfortunately, he spotted me, too, and, as soon as he looked up from the paper, I could see the panic on his face.

Quick as a flash, he went for the phone and, at that moment, I felt like doing a James Bond and going flying in straight through the plate-glass window. But still I would have been too late because I could see him mouthing the word 'police' down the telephone. He was about as scared as anyone I had ever seen, so I banged on the window shouting, 'I'm coming in to shoot you … I'm coming to shoot you.'

That's when Eddie pulled me away. 'The Old Bill will be here any minute,' he said. 'We've got to scarper.' So we both ran back to the car as fast as possible and drove off without even explaining to Nicole what had gone on.

When we were at a suitable nearby pub, we took out the guns and hid them underneath the bins at the side of the place.

'Right,' I said. 'Now we've got to go back to the house.'

'But that's madness,' replied Eddie. 'The Old Bill are going to be there.'

'Exactly. And if we don't go back and face them now, as if

nothing has happened, they are going to come looking for us, which will be much worse. Come on, you two, in the car.'

When we returned to the house, the scene was surreal. It was swarming with police, but we managed to walk up the driveway as nonchalantly as possible.

'There they are,' screamed Nicole's ex-boyfriend. 'There they are. They've come to kill me.'

One of the officers turned to me. 'Do you know this gentleman?' he asked.

'Yeah, we know him,' I replied.

'Well, he is making allegations that you have come to shoot him.'

'He's what?' I said as startled as possible.

'He says you were here earlier, threatening to kill him.'

I laughed and shrugged and then said to the copper, 'Officer, do you mind if I talk to you privately?'

We stepped out of earshot and I explained, 'We have actually come round to make sure he wasn't doing any harm to himself. I phoned him earlier to tell him we were on our way. And here we are. He has a very serious drugs problem, a very serious problem, and is taking a lot of medication. He suffers from delusions and even once threatened to kill the children of the lady who has accompanied us,' I continued, pointing to Nicole in the car. 'I wouldn't believe a word this man says. We are here to help and, obviously, if you wish to search us for any weapons or anything we don't mind. We have nothing to hide.'

Mentally, I was keeping my fingers crossed and I was rewarded when the police bought our story.

'I'm glad you've come forward, sir. We were going to order a helicopter search because of what this man is saying. If you'll just wait here a while, sir, I'll see if I can clear things up.'

We were kept waiting for about half-an-hour, and then the police let us go. But that wasn't the end of it as far as I was concerned. When I got back to Mottingham, it was about 3.00am and I was still fuming. A mate of mine, a really big gangster, phoned me by chance and we got talking about what had been going on that evening.

'But you must have revenge, Duchy. It is honour. It is your honour and that of Nicole,' he said with his Turkish accent. 'I will help you.'

The next thing I know, he's at the door with a mate of his and well tooled up with the iron bar from a dumbbell slipped down his trousers. He was accompanied by a friend and this time we went all the way back to Maidstone and, on the way, no one spoke a word to each other. This was serious business.

When we got to the house – for the third time in a night – my pal insisted I stay in the car.

'I bring you back a souvenir, my friend,' he said. 'A souvenir you will cherish.'

They smashed in the door of the house and I dread to think what went on after that, but they were gone quite a while and I could hear muffled screams even from as far away as the bottom of the driveway. I had been in fights all my life but these were tough, hardened gangsters who would stop at nothing.

After what seemed an age, they both came back down the drive and got in the car.

'You get no more trouble from him,' said my friend. 'Here is your souvenir.' And, with a smile, he handed over this huge molar, the tooth I wear round my neck on a gold chain to this day. I could barely speak. 'But why …' I started to say.

'Why, Duchy, why? Because we are Arifs and we live by a certain code.'

I have friends still in prison doing 14 years for having wars with the Arifs in the Old Kent Road. But for once I was glad they were on my side. They had smashed out all the teeth from a 35-year-old geezer using an iron bar from a dumbbell set. I was impressed.

After that, I did what I said I would never do, and acquired a gun for myself. It was for protection. My best friend Lee didn't like the idea and kept telling me to get rid of it. But I didn't want to because a friend of ours had recently been killed and I thought things might be hotting up.

* * *

At the time, in the early to mid-Nineties, Lydd Airport near Ashford in Kent was the scene for some of the most fantastic all-night raves in the main hangar and warehouse.

One night, I decided to go down there and I drove as fast as possible because you had to be there before midnight. I had my bird, my drugs and my gun – plus a few other bits and pieces.

I parked up and thought I'd have a smoke. So I was looking for a bit of 'rocky' I had in a bag when the bird I was with said, 'Hey, Duch, there's a policeman looking at you.'

By the time I'd glanced up from searching for the rocky, there were seven of them advancing towards the vehicle.

'Do you mind stepping out of the car, sir?' said one of them as politely as possible. I swung my legs over and lifted myself through the door frame. One of them started patting me down.

'Hey, what's going on here?' I exclaimed.

'Just a precaution, sir.'

And then he found the knife that I had sewn into my leather jacket and raised his eyebrows a little.

'Do you have any other stickers with you?' he asked.

'Nah, just that. That's my knife … I never go anywhere without it.'

Without changing his polite manner, the copper said, 'This gentleman has a knife. Could someone please cuff him.'

'Woah … woah,' I said. 'Slow down. Can't we sort something out?'

One of the other Old Bill said, 'We have an amnesty box. If you put whatever drugs you are holding and your knife in the box then you can carry on and enjoy yourself.'

I was just about to do that when one of the other Old Bill shouted, 'Sarge, Sarge. He's got a gun round here.'

That's when I knew I was done for.

I had slipped the gun down the side of my seat in the car when I was looking for the rocky. With any luck it should never have been seen. But some fucking eagle-eyed boy scout had found it.

Two coppers went to grab me as the boy scout opened the gun he had picked up and said, 'Guv, this gun's loaded.'

'Do you have anything to say, sir?' said the sergeant, still with his polite voice.

'Well, yeah. I mean, I don't know anyone who carries a gun who doesn't carry it loaded.'

I was arrested and taken to a mobile police station where I demanded a doctor, a solicitor and everything.

The police took my puff. They took my whiz. They already had the knife and a big spike they found concealed in my crutch. Then there was the bag of cartridges and, of course, the gun.

'You're either a drug-dealer, an arms seller or a hit-man … which one are you?' asked one of the officers.

I thought, Christ, I'm all three if you like. But instead I replied, 'You've been watching too much fucking television.'

And they carted me off to the nick.

I knew that I'd messed things up badly this time and let everyone down. But my dad came to see me when I was on remand and he shocked me by saying, 'Well, son, you've said people have tried to kill you before so maybe you needed the gun for protection.'

From that moment on, me and Dad were really tight.

When I came up before the beak, I couldn't believe what was happening. I hadn't been in serious trouble for years and the judge said he was taking that into consideration. So, when he sentenced me to four years in prison, I thought he must have been talking about someone behind me. I instinctively turned round to see who it might be.

But the only face I saw was that of my dad who winked as if to say, 'Keep strong, son.'

'Take him down,' were the last words I heard.

13

Whole Again

I'D HIT ANOTHER low ebb in my life, probably my lowest. Just as I had finally been accepted by my parents – my father especially – I'd gone and messed everything up again.

And this time Belmarsh was hard, very hard. Like all prisons, this allocation nick in South London, even though relatively new, hadn't been designed with disabled prisoners in mind. So instead of being put on one of the wings, or 'house blocks' as they call them, I was immediately assigned to the healthcare unit.

'Hey, mate,' I asked one of the screws, 'why am I being put in here? I'm not ill.'

'For a start, my name's not "mate". And you are here because you're not A1. You're not full-bodied ... you're disabled.'

'Yeah, well, that ain't an illness, you know.'

'Maybe, but we haven't got anywhere else to put you.'

Most people probably think life on the healthcare block is cushy. That's why some prisoners would harm themselves, cut themselves, to try and hang out there as long as they could. They'd look upon it as a little holiday from the rest of the prison.

But it was no such thing. It might be OK for a couple of days if you had a cold but, if you had to stay there for months like I did, it would begin to rot your brain.

For a start, there was no gym to help me keep in shape, and there was no access to education. On the blocks, it was different. In house block two, the drug-free unit, you were out of your cell and you were working, getting a bit more spending cash. House block three you didn't bother with, it was called Beirut and it was a shit-hole, no toilet paper, a hell-hole.

The only thing the healthcare block had going for itself was TV in the afternoon and if you've seen afternoon TV, you'll know why I wanted out.

I'd shout at the screws, 'Hey, I thought this was an allocation nick. When am I being sent to a proper prison?'

'When somebody wants you … now shut up, Peter.'

Prisons could easily be adapted for disabled cons. All you need is a lift, one or two cells with extra-wide doors for wheelchairs, and maybe a ramp or two.

But the way the authorities looked at it they wouldn't even fit ramps because when able-bodied people walk up ramps they can hurt themselves, so it's a liability.

On top of my frustration about being unable to use the gym and not being able to study anything, I found myself in the health block surrounded by nutters. And, if it wasn't nutters, it was nonces. One bloke was in there because he was badly burned down his face and his body. He told me it had happened after he nicked a car and then crashed it. I found out later that it wasn't true. He was a nonce and the guys that had set him on fire were on house block three. The story was that he had shacked up with this bird and started interfering with her kids. The kids told their mum, she told her brother, her brother told her dad and – well, you can guess what happened next. They've gone round there with a can of petrol and set the cunt alight. The mad thing is that he'll get time off for that.

I tried again by pleading to be put on another block, but I was rejected every time.

'We can't help you, Peter,' would be the standard reply. 'We don't have facilities for the likes of you on the blocks. Don't you understand? Disabled people aren't supposed to come to prison.'

I met Baz again in Belmarsh. Things had gone bad for Baz. He had gone back to the Charlie in a big way and now he was bang on the brown, on the heroin. I also heard he had grassed me and the boys up over the skunk operation. That's something you should never do when you work with me. Not ever.

Most people spend a maximum of three months in Belmarsh and then they are allocated to another prison where they usually serve out the rest of their sentence.

But not me. Three months rolled by … then four months … five months. By this time, I was getting really depressed, it was really starting to get me down. I've never been much of a letter-writer, not even to my family or mates, but I decided the only way I could be taken seriously was if I wrote to the Home Office to plead my case. And that's exactly what I did. I said I was being punished twice. Once for the crime I had committed and again because I had no gym, no education and no access to facilities.

Now I had another disappointment– no reply. That made matters worse, and I started to worry.

Because I was getting no help with adjusting my offending

behaviour, no help with anger management, no drug rehabilitation programme or anything else, I feared that, when I did eventually come up for parole, I wouldn't get that either because I hadn't done any of those things.

It was starting to do my head in. It was like I was caught in a vicious circle and there was no one around to help.

I wrote to my MP, Bridget Prentice, but she couldn't do a lot, and so I wrote to Anne Widdecombe who was then the Minister at the Home Office with responsibility for prisons and immigration.

And this time I got a reply.

But, as usual, Anne Widdecombe had got the wrong end of the stick. In essence she said, 'Up yours ... you've been caught with guns before and so Belmarsh is the perfect place for you, young man.'

For one thing, I hadn't been caught with guns before and, for another, the health block at Belmarsh was anywhere but the best place for me.

I was sinking into despair. That was when I decided I would go on hunger-strike.

One frustrated nurse called June, God bless her, came up to me and said, 'Please don't do this, please don't. It'll get you nowhere.'

'Well, nothing else has got me anywhere, has it?' I replied.

'But you're harming yourself ... what's the point?'

But I was determined. There was a point and I had to prove it for me and for any future disabled prisoners who might find themselves in Belmarsh.

But the nurse was having none of it and she enlisted the help of a screw called B.A., Buzz Alan. He was OK – for a screw – and he was the first person in that nick who sat down and actually listened to what I was saying. All the others just dismissed me as if I was crazy.

'And just what do you think you'll get out of all this, Peter?' he asked.

'Somebody to take what I'm saying seriously. I've been in the health block of an allocation nick for nearly a year. I'm not ill. I'm only supposed to be in this nick for three months at the most, and no way am I being taught how to build a new life. Nobody stands a fighting fucking chance in here.'

And the screw listened.

Then he said, 'Peter, one day you'll get out of this experience and then you can campaign for disabled people's rights in prison. But you ain't going to do it if you're a bag of dead bones. Don't think for one moment you'll get away with a hunger-strike. The truth is that nobody really cares if you do die. Now think about it.'

And I did. And I realised he was right. I was better alive and campaigning, so I called off my hunger-strike.

Then I started writing to everyone. The late Bernie Grant MP got a letter. I was firing them off left, right and centre. I was worried sick that without any rehabilitation I wouldn't get my parole. I wrote to the Prisons Ombudsman, anyone I could think of.

The exercise yard in Belmarsh was the only place I could walk but it was one of the most appalling places I had ever seen. It was small, only about 20ft by 20ft, no greenery and just a tiny bit of blue sky overhead. But worst of all, the yard was covered in shit. Apart from the pigeon shit and the stench of dead mice, there were all the human shit parcels thrown out of the windows by prisoners who were banged up. It was the most disgusting place I had ever seen and I swore I'd never go outside until I could touch grass and smell the outdoors again instead of someone else's crap.

Then, one morning, my cell was opened at about 7.00am,

which is very unusual because nothing begins on that block until about 8.30am.

'Peter,' said the screw, 'there is someone here to see you.'

And in strode this very smartly dressed woman from the Prison Ombudsman's office. I knew that finally the shit had hit the fan when she immediately started apologising.

'We were under the impression that you had been reallocated months and months ago,' she said with what seemed like genuine concern. 'I'm shocked that you are still here. I'll try and make sure that something is done about it straight away.'

'You mean I'll finally get on to one of the other house blocks?' I muttered despondently.

'Oh no, no not at all. I mean to get you out of here.'

And she was as good as her word. Seven days later, I was on my way to Her Majesty's Prison Send, Ripley Road, Woking, Surrey. It was like a breath of fresh air.

I had been held in Belmarsh for 16 months.

I've since found out that it was not totally the fault of the Belmarsh authorities that I was left to languish on the healthcare block for all that time. They can only re-allocate prisoners to a nick that wants to take them. And, if you are disabled, then nobody wants to take you because there are no facilities. To put it bluntly, cripples are considered a liability in the prison system. But that doesn't excuse Belmarsh. Nothing does. In a way, I knew that I would miss the steady pace of control at Belmarsh, and June, Buzz and the PO, Mr Firefield, the ones that gave me a fighting chance.

Send was a 'C' category prison which had originally been built as a smallpox isolation hospital. Because I was now a 'C' category prisoner, it meant I could go out at weekends. But I still felt alienated and experienced massive culture-shock because of my experiences in Belmarsh. Seeing my kids, Jade and Dean, helped make up for things, even though the relationship I was in at the time, with a girl called Kirsten, seemed to me to be going pear-shaped. There's one thing that runs through all prisoners' heads when they're in the nick – is my other half seeing someone else while I'm banged up?

But I couldn't dwell on it because there were so many people to see in the couple of days I was out of prison.

I knew I should go and see my mum and dad because they had stuck by me. But I was embarrassed and kept putting it off. Instead, I went to see my old mates and that's when Jimmy told me that the firm had all but disbanded since I'd gone inside.

'It's been a long time, Duch,' he said. 'You were the only one who could keep the old firm together. They've all drifted off and gone their own ways now. It'll be easy to get them back together, though, if you like … it could be just like the old days when you get out for good.'

'No, Jimmy, that's not what I want at all. I don't want to go back to the old days.'

He looked at me quizzically. 'You going straight, Duch?'

'Come on, Jimmy, you know me better than that.'

But he didn't.

While I was in Send, I met a guy who was inside on fraud charges. He was one of the most cultured people I had ever met. He was also one of the richest in the prison. He went to work every day in London and came back at night to be locked up. He fascinated me. The story was that he had fraudulently evaded more than £200m of taxes. He was a hero because anyone who could stick it that far up the Inland Revenue was bound to be a hero.

One day, I got talking to him and told him that I was interested in music. Then I plucked up enough courage to give him a copy of my CD. I didn't think much about it until he approached me a few days later and said, 'Duch, that music of yours is really good, very professional. I enjoyed listening to it.'

'You're only saying that.'

'No, I'm not. I know a bit about the music business.'

'Well, that's very kind,' I said, not thinking what else to say.

'In fact, I've got an entertainment company and I might be able to give you a job on the days they allow you out of here.'

I was gobsmacked.

The company specialised, as it does today, in booking tribute bands. There would be lookalike Spice Girls acts, musicians who looked and sounded like Queen and hundreds more. My job was to keep the bookings coming in. I had my own phone, a computer, keys to the office, everything. Slowly, I was becoming a different person.

I'd enjoy getting dressed up and going to work. Even the screws used to rib me, saying, 'Who do you think you are dressed like that, Duchy? The Governor?'

While at work, I was able to get my own music punted out a bit by ringing up the right people.

The Governor was only too pleased that I was getting work experience and I was allowed out of prison five days a week. I had to pay the prison £40 out of my pay, and whatever else I earned I could give to my family. In fact, I was one of the few people sending money to their families because most of the people had to rely on money being sent in to them.

But, when I went back into prison, I wasn't allowed to take any money with me and that included bank cards and the like.

It was just a few weeks to go before my parole when I went back into prison after a weekend home visit. I had been using a bank card on the outside to get cash for food while I was working and this particular weekend I'd smoked a couple of spliffs with a few mates. I didn't worry about it because I'd had drug tests at the prison before and they had all been negative, so I thought a little smoke on a Friday night would be all right. By Monday morning, it would be out of my system and I would be sweet.

Something must have happened at Send over the weekend because, by the time I got back, security was a lot more rigorous.

As I entered the prison, a screw said, 'All right, Peter?'

'Yeah, fine.'

'Just roll up your trouser leg, please.'

'Why's that?'

'Just do as you're told.'

So I did it and showed him my artificial legs. The screw gave them a cursory glance and said, 'You're clear, Peter ... go on.'

As I entered the waiting room rolling my trouser legs back down, one of the other screws noticed and said, 'Good idea them legs, ain't they? Very clever ... how are they built?'

'They're made from titanium, like on the spaceships,' I said. 'I get 'em done over in Dulwich, South London, a place called King's College.'

'Very smart.'

And, as I lifted up a bit of sponge to show him the titanium frame, I nearly shit myself. There was a 50p piece just sitting there.

He saw it and, in true screw fashion, said, 'What's being going on here, then?'

Next thing I knew, he had pulled out the sponge and found the bank card and a piece of puff. I was nicked.

I lost my job and it looked likely I was going to lose my parole as well. I had no one else to blame but myself, so I blamed myself heavily. I spent about a week sitting in my cell thinking, You stupid idiot. With just a few more days to go to your parole, you've buggered everything up, and now they can nick you for another two months on top of your sentence.

What was it about me? It was almost as if I had a self-destructive streak. No sooner had my father finally accepted me for who I was than I got banged up again. Now I was within days of release and there I go again. I wondered whether I'd become institutionalised because of all the places I'd been in during my life, from children's homes to borstals and prisons. But I couldn't figure it out. All I knew was that I was being sent straight back to Belmarsh.

I kept telling myself not to worry. I had done it now and there was no use in worrying. There were lots of geezers who had got so far, then fucked it up at the end and lost their parole. I wasn't alone.

I was hauled up before the Governor.

'I'm disappointed in you, Peter.'

'Yes, sir, I know, sir.'

'I never expected to see you back here. I thought that, after all the time you had spent here, you wouldn't want to come back.'

'I didn't want to, sir.'

Then he looked down and flicked through a file he had on his desk.

'Mmm,' he said. 'Are you still using dihydrocodeine? The DF 118s, I mean.'

'No, sir.'

'Are you telling the truth?'

'Yes, sir.'

'Then why the cannabis?'

And so I explained to the Governor that I had become addicted to dihydrocodeine, which is an opiate-based painkiller, because of my disability. But I had managed to kick the habit by going cold turkey and the one way in which I managed to stay off DF 118 tablets was by smoking puff. I came clean and told him that I'd never made any secret about smoking dope but that I was completely detoxed as far as the dihydrocodeine went.

'Well, at least I admire your frankness, Peter,' he said. 'And I am going to give you one more chance. But this will be your very last chance. If I were you, I would grasp it and hold on to it as strongly as you can. Have I made myself clear?'

'Yes, sir.'

'Your parole stands.'

And so it was that, on 14 April 1998, I was finally freed.

I didn't want to go home to Mottingham, because I knew there was something not right about my relationship with Kirsten and I didn't want to face the truth, the possibility that she might have someone else.

If she had been cheating on me then the door was wide open for me to go back to Belmarsh. There was no way I was going to let a woman cheat on me while I had been banged up and, if that was the case, she would get what was coming to her and damn the consequences.

But I tried to hold on to the Governor's words. This was my very last chance. So I went away to Hertfordshire for two weeks and stayed with friends. Then I moved down to Swanley for a couple of nights. But I knew that I was only postponing the inevitable and, one night at about 11.30pm, I said to my mate Lee, 'Take me home, I've got to find out for myself what's going on.'

I rang the bell but no one answered the door.

'Kirsten,' I shouted. 'Kirsten, it's me … Duchy.' Still no answer.

So I decided to go round the back and see if I could get in that way. As I passed by the living-room window, I saw someone hurriedly draw the curtain across.

'Kirsten,' I shouted again. 'Are you there?'

Getting no answer, I broke the window in the kitchen door and let myself in. And there she was, standing in front of me, all flustered.

'Duchy,' she said, 'why didn't you phone and tell me you was out? This is a surprise.'

'I bet.'

I stomped straight into the bedroom and there he was sitting on her little boy's bed.

'Who the fuck are you?' I shouted.

'I'm Del … Delroy,' he replied sheepishly, eyes darting everywhere.

'And who are you to her?'

But, before he could reply, Kirsten answered from behind me. 'I'm seeing him,' she said.

I spun round.

For two seconds a flash went through my mind. When I was in Send, I remembered me and my mate watching this guy in a phone box screaming down the phone to his wife, 'You fucking slag. If you go out tonight, I'm going to fucking kill you.' He said to me, 'You know what, Duchy, this guy's doing a nine and he's on his last bit of bird. But he's the sort of guy that'll get released tomorrow, go home, find his wife's been unfaithful, kill her stone dead and get a life sentence.'

But I was boiling with rage, life sentence or no fucking life sentence. And so I lifted my hand up to smash her one … but then there was a sudden calm in my head. Instead of laying into her, I used my arm to point at the door.

'Not in my house,' I shouted. 'Not in my house you're not seeing him. Now you get out of here. Take your little boyfriend and your fucking kid and piss off out of here. And I never ever want to see you again. Get out!'

It was about 3.00am and I threw them all out on the streets. When they had gone, I sat down and, for the first time in my life, I felt really composed. Instead of fucking everything up like I usually do, I had done the right thing. I'd done the right bloody thing.

And that's what changed my world around. I'd saved myself from going back to Belmarsh. I wasn't institutionalised, I wasn't a victim of my own anger, I did have a future, and I did have a family. And I had one last fighting chance to prove to the world that I could make it.

There was the small problem of my parole officer, of course. If she knew what I had done she would have reported that I didn't have a stable home to live in. So I decided to keep stum for a while. Later, I told my friends that Kirsten and I had split up, but the truth was that I had kicked her out to save myself. Eventually, the parole officer did get to know, but she was sympathetic. She said she knew it must have been hard for me to keep calm after all the time I had spent in the nick. That was when I knew I wasn't the same man I used to be and that I had changed for good.

I thought I'd had a chance to change my life before with my ambition to be a pop star. And, although everyone supported me, it always kept coming to nothing. All I ever seemed to do was let people down. But this time I swore that, if I could just be given one more chance, I would show the world what I was made of.

The first thing I had to do with my new life was get the band back together, and the second thing I had to do was get a job.

The job arrived first.

A mate of mine named Mark had started a building company which he ran solely on a computer, very impressive. I said to him, 'If you've got a project, a house to build or something like that, I can get stuck in and get the guys to come and build it for you.'

And that's how a company called TDB & Co started. It was short for The Dog's Bollocks, and Charlie the roofer was involved along with Mickey Amos, Charlie's wife and half the workers from Lewisham Council.

Once the company was up and running, I decided it was time to go and see my parents again.

At first, my dad was a bit apprehensive and I didn't blame him after all I had put him through. But we warmed to each other. It was all small-talk.

'I see the roof's still holding up then, Dad.'

'It's fine, son, thanks to you and Charlie.'

'I'm working with a building company meself now, Dad,' I said.

'Oh yes, and what are they called?'

'TDB & Co, over Lewisham way.'

'I'm glad to hear you've got a proper job, Raymond. What does TDB stand for?'

'Oh, nothing,' I stuttered, 'just the owner's name, I think.'

It was nice to be back with Mum and Dad, having Sunday lunch again, and finally being a real family.

I was the production manager at the company and I learned the trade. I learned how to do architraving, tiling and all the other things. But I knew that TDB wasn't going to last for ever and, when the inevitable came and the company closed down, I was scared of being unemployed in case it led me back to crime. I needed a job, any job, to reassure myself that I wasn't institutionalised.

And that's when the maddest thing happened. I did something I said I'd never do – I got a job on the doors. A friend of mine, Lin, said I should go and talk to a guy called Syd over at a club called Sahara's in Lewisham, who said he knew me. She was talking to an old mate of mine and when I got down there: Big Lloyd, Mackie Keith Price, Micky D, all the old guys from back in the day were down there. That's when I met this guy they all respected called Stilks. He had the mightiest reputation in clubland and was, without a doubt, Britain's hardest bouncer. Throughout his years on the doors, the scum had thrown the lot at him – knives, guns, chains, you name it.

He had never been beaten and the way he dealt with troublemakers was to either smash them to pieces or quietly put them to sleep with the 'Stilks Stranglehold'.

He was a martial arts expert, tall, tough, hard as nails and disgustingly fit. No wonder the first time he cast eyes on me, he said, 'Oh yeah, now here's another runt I've got to fucking look after.'

'Don't worry about me, mate,' I said. 'If there's any trouble, I'll give 'em two pounds for their trousers and fight them for their tie. I can bench press 150kg – three times me own body weight.'

'You're having a laugh, ain't ya?' replied Stilks. 'I do weight-lifting and three times your body weight is impossible.'

'OK, I bet you I can. I'll prove it.'

So we shook on it in front of all the other bouncers and I realised there was no going back.

I had to train for about six weeks before I was ready to meet Stilks down the gym. It had been years since I had been a lifting champion and the months in prison with no gym had taken their toll. But I worked hard and worked consistently to get all my strength back.

251

The day of the lift, I got there early to compose myself. In walked Stilks. 'Watcha waitin' for?' he said. 'Get on with it.'

And I did. My biceps were pumped up like rugby balls as Stilks spotted for me from behind and I lay down on the bench. The grim determination made the veins on my forehead stand out, and slowly, slowly I lifted the 150kg into the air. The pain was enormous, the concentration intense as my elbows locked and I held the weights aloft.

Stilks was blown away and just kept shaking his head in disbelief. So, just to rub things in a bit, I bench-pressed the weight another couple of times.

Since then, Stilks has called me his hero and we have become the very best of mates. But he liked to remind me, 'If it goes off, remember I'll always get to the door first.'

One day, it did go off. Three guys came down from Brixton and a disagreement ensued about how they were dressed and one thing and another. So they mouthed off and said they'd be coming back. With the experience I had of Brixton blokes, I thought they could easily go and get their guns and someone would end up hurt. So I kept my eye on the door monitor and, about 20 minutes later, I saw three figures approaching.

I grabbed my crutches and shot down the stairs, almost knocking Stilks over. I winked at him. He didn't think I could move that fast.

I collared the first of the three blokes. 'I know what you've come back for, but you ain't coming in here. Now hop it.'

'Yeah, and what you gonna do, you fucking cripple?' he laughed as Stilks went up to say something to them.

'I'm gonna do this,' I replied, and with that I lifted up my crutch and thrashed him around the head. As I saw the blood starting to trickle down his face, I spun round as quickly as possible to hit another one and watch his head split open.

'I hate being called cripple,' I said with a wide, false smile.

The third geezer shit himself and ran in front of Stilks to hide. So I leaned over Stilks's shoulder, tried to imagine where the guy would be and smashed my crutch down. They all ran off shouting and screaming.

'That was unbelievable,' said Stilks. 'All I saw was your arm come over me shoulder, Duch, and you cracked him right on his head. Wow. What a fuckin' shot, all I saw was the blood run down his face. But don't you ever get to the fucking door again first,' he laughed. 'That's my job.'

When I started the door work, there was a bloke named Tony Ellen there who was also a martial artist. I'd known him years ago when I was doing me *nunchukas* training with Bob McCormack and Bob Chaproniere. We had promised to stay in touch but we never had. And now, after all this time, we bumped into each other again. I didn't even recognise him at first.

When he wasn't on the doors, Tony would give martial arts demonstrations at different places. 'You ought to do that, Duchy,' he said one day. 'You'd be bloody good with your skills.'

And that's how I started out giving demonstrations on the use of *nunchukas* and how versatile they were as a martial arts weapon. My fame started to grow a little, thanks to Tony Ellen and friends, and soon I was being interviewed for *Combat* magazine and the reporter asked me what I did in my spare time.

'Music and that,' I said.

The guy was interested and so I gave him a copy of my CD. I had managed to put Harlequin back together and we had been in the studio to do some more stuff. Lody down at the club had a partner called Martin and together they ran a management company and with their help, I managed to make my own small documentary, although it's still waiting to be broadcast.

Things were starting to look up. And, after I appeared on the TV series *Hard Bastards*, I decided to give up the door work for a while and try to promote myself on the telly.

First stop was *Big Brother*. I decided to write to the show's producers out of the blue. I thought that was the best way to go. They wanted something different on *Big Brother* and, well … I'm something more than just different.

I went for an interview in North London to get on the show and even the guy on the door recognised me.

'Hey, ain'tcha that bloke that was on the telly? What was it now … that *Hard Bastards* show?'

'Yeah,' I said, feeling real cool.

This *Big Brother*, I thought, should be no problem at all. No problem whatsoever.

But I shouldn't have been so cocky. One of the producers was a fairly bossy woman, ordering people about, and telling everyone what to do. She came straight up to me and said out loud so everyone else could hear, 'I'm sorry, but we are going to do something that involves legs now so you won't be able to do this. You just sit there.'

I had never been so cruelly dismissed or so downhearted and hurt. It affected me big-time and I wanted to leave right there and then because I knew there was no way now they were going to pick me for the show. I wondered why they had bothered to invite me to the auditions in the first place.

The task they had picked for the hopefuls involved a rowing machine. When I saw that was all it was, I protested to the woman producer, 'I can do that easily.'   'I'm afraid you can't,' she replied patronisingly.

'Yes, I can. I can use my hands just as well as able-bodied people use their feet. Let me show you.'

But she wouldn't let me show her and she made it plain she thought I would have a problem with all the tasks on the show. If they had let me continue, then I am sure I could have made an impact on how people with disabilities are seen and judged. But I was shell-shocked by their attitude. It reminded me of that old manager we had, who was always warning me that showbusiness didn't like disabled people. Performers always had to be wholesome and able-bodied. Maybe he had a point after all.

Big Brother had very rigid ideas about people and I realised that it wasn't my scene. But I wasn't disheartened for too long and I set my sights on the BBC show *Fame Academy.*

I reckoned that all the people who appeared on shows like that, even the ones who didn't win, usually ended up with some kind of record deal. And that's what I was after. You'd see all the contestants upset when they were knocked off the show but I'd think, Shut up, you soppy cunt, you're made, you've got it made, you'll get a contract.

There was one problem with *Fame Academy.* They only wanted performers up to the age of 35 and I was 39. But I thought I'd go for it anyway and just lie about my age. I imagined winning and then saying, 'I don't want this win … I'll give it to the contestant down from me because I'm 40.' I thought of all sorts of daft things.

When I arrived at the Novotel in London for the open auditions, there were thousands and thousands of other hopefuls queuing right round the building and my heart sank. I was miles from the front of the queue. Then I spotted this black guy who was controlling the crowd.

'Hey, mate,' I yelled, 'I've got to stand in this queue on me crutches. Any chance I can just go in there, do me audition and leave?'

'I'll see what can be done,' he replied.

Obviously, it wasn't much because, a couple of hours later, I was still standing there and things were getting so bad they were auditioning people in the street.

Then the black guy reappeared and escorted me to the front of the queue and into the hotel. 'I've been looking for you,' he said. 'You can go in now if you want.'

It was a great pleasure walking past all the other hopefuls but, when I got to the desk inside the hotel, I started to get a bit nervous. I gave them all my particulars – including my age as 35 – and I started to relax a bit. I tuned my guitar to perfection, took a deep breath and went into the audition room where I sang a song I'd written for my new girlfriend, Jane, called 'Again'.

I played the song with confidence and then had to wait another couple of hours to find out whether I had got through to the next round.

When I heard that I had, I couldn't wipe the grin off my face for ages. I was told to come back the next day with another song prepared for a final audition.

I agonised about which song to perform, and decided on an old U2 favourite, 'With or Without You'.

Crunch time was here. I was relaxed and again confident as I approached the judging panel. Then I went for it.

I hit the notes perfectly. I soared on the lines, 'I can't live, with or without you ...' And the guitar work was faultless with perfect chord changes.

When I finished, there was silence and I thought, Oh God, I've blown it.

Then one of the judges started clapping, and then another. Clat ... clat ... clat ... clat ...

I'd done it, I'd got there. It was the sound of applause.

Epilogue

OBVIOUSLY, THEY SUSSED ME OUT.

The show's bosses sent me a letter with the address of the place where *Fame Academy* was going to be recorded and they also asked for proof of my age. Evidently, they had checked on the electoral roll and had found out that I was 40. It didn't match with their record of me being 35 and I was given 24 hours to sort out the discrepancy.

I had no alternative but to go and see them and put my hand up. They were good about it and said it was a real shame they had to disqualify me. But I had beaten 12,000 other people to get where I was, so that was some compensation.

'We really enjoyed auditioning you and had great hopes for you,' one of the judges said.

But I couldn't let things drop without a parting shot. 'I didn't realise fame and talent don't count if you are over 35,'